"*AWAKE!* is a powerful journey of the heart. It is evidence of the power of love to shed light in dark places. This book will encourage you to stand in the balance between faith and love so that you can truly live in the Kingdom."

– Bob Mumford, Lifechangers, Fort Lauderdale, Florida –

"Valid testimony always enhances the value of past experiences, but it also releases the present power of Jesus. In her testimony, Roxy Lynch declares there is more to being born again than an experience. It is a walk, a witness, and a war. And the war is winnable because Jesus has already won it. Roxy has not been afraid to share the 'tough stuff' in sharing her testimony of victory in her marriage against seemingly impossible odds. Besides being a simple, hard-hitting account of walking with Jesus amid pain, this book is a report on the faithfulness of God. It is also proof of what happens when one stands in stubborn, relentless faith that God can redeem and restore a marriage as well as prepare and anoint for ministry. It is happening even now in the lives of Roxy and Mike Lynch. This book stands as a challenge to live the Kingdom life. This is a good read for a new Christian, for those who need to begin anew in their God-walk, and for the rest of us who always can stand fresh inspiration."

– Jack Taylor, President, Dimensions Ministries, Melbourne, Florida –

"Roxy Lynch writes her story as a precursor to a new gracious nature. Further, you will see the impact of love on what the church might define as losers. Only in Roxy's story, it was not just the stranger that she had to decide to love; it was one very dear to her. She relays what grace and mercy, faith, and love can do to change one heart, a heart that will then impact cities and nations simply because it has experienced receiving love and offered grace. Roxy understands the power of the 'story.' It is a very personal journey about the faithfulness of God as she describes real-life issues with no holds barred and then tells how her life was transformed over the years and what God used in her life. You will find yourself, your life, a piece of your journey somewhere in this story; a place where you can be comforted, find hope, or know how one person made their way through a dark place. Maybe you will find yourself in place of needing to give grace; needing to receive grace."

– David VanCronkhite, Blood N Fire, Atlanta, Georgia –

AWAKE!

Arise From The Dead
And Walk As Children Of Light

By Roxy Lynch

Forward by James W. Goll

To order copies of this book or contact Roxy and BNF Ministries, see web.me.com/bnfmpls or email bnfmpls@me.com.

THANK YOU!

Mom for your determination to be strong in hard times. Thanks also for pre-proofreading this book.

My most favorite person in the whole wide world, my Mikey. Thank you for your loving-kindness toward me and for always seeing the best in me. I am so proud of you and I love you dearly and forever!!

My children, Michael Jr., Rachael, and Janell for hearing our story, forgiving us, and being willing to share us with many others who are walking through difficult times. I am proud of each of you and I love you forever!

My son-in-law, Joe, who is fighting for our country in the United States Marine Corp. I am proud of you, Son, and I love you. Thanks for being anxious to read this book also.

Our spiritual daughter, Victoria. God has taught me as much as you as we walk through your road to freedom from all your past into your destiny. You are becoming a mighty woman of God and VICTORY IS IMMINENT!

My sister, Sue Torguson. How can I thank you for putting your heart and soul into painting the eye for the cover (which is 30 inches in real life). What a blessing your successful efforts are to me. Thank you so much. I love you!

David Sluka for your help getting this book completed and published.

Thomas Neel for the great cover design.

Jack Taylor, Bob Mumford, David VanCronkhite, and James Goll, thank you for taking the time to read this book and share recommendations and James for writing the forward. I cannot express my humble gratitude for your time!

Thanks and praise always to my God who has so tenderly walked me through many difficulties showing me my faults, teaching me to how to change and how to love.

ISBN-10: 0-615-30200-9
ISBN-13: 978-0-615-30200-3

Printed in the United States of America

For you were once darkness,
but now you are light in the Lord.

Walk as children of light…

AWAKE

You who sleep, arise from the dead,
and Christ will give you light.

Ephesians 5:8, 14

TABLE OF CONTENTS

FORWARD BY JAMES W. GOLL

AWAKE! — CHOOSE RIGHT!

In this hour the Holy Spirit has a strategic word He is releasing. Through the confirmation of many voices He is saying it is time for us to WAKE UP! Roxy Lynch is another one of those voices God is speaking to loud and clear in this hour. It is time for an awakening to occur in the Body of Christ to let our light penetrate this present darkness. This book will help you to choose your way wisely so that you can fully walk in God's assignment for you.

Let me share with you a dream that confirms the contents of this wonderful book you have in your hands. Recently I was given a message that came in the form of a vivid, yet simple dream. It was a Matrix-type dream – similar in style to the *Matrix* movie series. In that series of movies the characters had a "red" or "blue" pill to choose between – and it was very important which pill you chose. You wanted to be on the right side of the force after all.

I had actually "awakened" early that particular morning and then I felt from the Holy Spirit that I was to linger in bed for a moment. Suddenly, it seemed, that I fell into a deep sleep and was given the following impacting revelatory encounter. Then I was awakened right at the exact right time – just in time to get ready for my appointment to teach that day. I woke up just in time! Now for the dream itself!

In this dream, two closed-fisted hands turned downward came before me. I knew that within each fist there was some type of important message. I knew it was important that I chose correctly. I pondered what I should do. A voice came to me and said, "Make your choice." I looked at both hands being offered and I heard myself say, "I choose right. I choose the right hand!"

The right hand then turned over in the dream and the fingers opened up. Contained within the palm of the hand was a white capsule. I watched as the white pill filled with heaven's ingredients and realms of glistening glory was placed in my right hand. Instinctively, I began to bring the white pill to my mouth. As I did so, I saw that there was a word written upon the pill. The word was "AWAKE."

As I put the Awake pill in my mouth in the dream, suddenly I woke up in the natural. The room was filled with the presence of the fear of the Lord. I intuitively knew that it was very important in the days that lie ahead that we make wise life choices centered around the fear of the Lord.

Let me summarize this dream for you:

1. It is important that we choose right!
2. It is important that we choose righteousness.
3. It is important that we choose to find our pleasures at the right hand of God almighty – in His son Jesus Christ.
4. It is important that we choose heavenly nutrients to feed our entire beings in these days.
5. We must feed ourselves the Word of purity.
6. We must see our present trials as tools of preparation for the days that lie ahead and choose the right course of action!
7. We must shake ourselves out of our slumber.
8. We must AWAKE!
9. By choosing wisely we will be ready just in time for our next assignment in God!

Like Roxy, I want to the body of Christ awakened and see Jesus receive the rewards of His suffering. I trust that this little dream has been meaningful for you. It has been helpful to me. I am really leaning on Jesus to wake me up where I have fallen asleep. How about you? It is time to be wide AWAKE!

Choosing Righteousness!

James W. Goll
Founder of Encounters Network
Author of *The Seer, The Coming Prophetic Revolution,*
Praying for Israel's Destiny, Dream Language and many others

INTRODUCTION

This book was written because I had a dream. Out of the dream God spoke to me about writing a book. I had no idea how to write a book, I don't even like to read (except my Bible), but... God said so, so I figured I better think about it seriously.

For near three years prior to this dream, things had been extremely difficult financially. We had been on missionary support for 11 years at the time and funds were low, to say the least. It seemed to make sense in the natural to get a job. I kept asking the Lord if I could and He kept saying, "No, keep doing what you're doing and trust Me!" What I was doing was, studying, teaching and counseling.

A couple months after the dream I made an office for myself to write. Clueless of what I would write about, I sat down at my desk one day, ready to write. I looked at my three years worth of study notes, along with words and dreams God had given us (my husband and I), all put into notebooks, and a light bulb went off. I realized it was all part of the plan. Almost every note in those notebooks went into this book.

I have written this out of my deep passion to see God's people wake up and see God's plan for them, that they have purpose here and now. I myself wasted so many years, not understanding that I was a dead-works Christian. I was born again, but sleepwalking through it seeing no change in my life. Through many trials and errors God has guided me into an incredible intimate relationship with Him.

Part 1 of this book shares my journey, which I was not going to put in the book, but God again guiding me, told me to do so. Part 2 is simple guidance for you, the reader, to hopefully help you find your way to walking in your destiny. Each chapter in this book could have its own book, but I wrote as I like to read a book, simple and to the point allowing the Holy Spirit room to teach.

I encourage you as you read to dig deep on your own and see what God may be personally saying to you. I pray He will give you wisdom and revelation to understand what His will and purpose are for you.

OOPS, CORRECTION!
The name of the movie in the 1st paragraph was
"A Thief in the Night", not "Left Behind"
Sorry for the confusion right off the bat :)

PART ONE:

MY BORN AGAIN EXPERIENCE
AND TESTIMONY

When I was a child, I can remember giving my life to the Lord every year at Bible camp. I would then do it again a couple months later when my church would show the movie *Left Behind*, where people would get their heads chopped off for not denying Christ. For those of you who did not have this scary experience as a child, this movie was about the rapture. People were left on earth because they were not "born again." Afterwards, through much trial and tribulation, they became Christians, and eventually were put to the chopping block and given a choice to deny Christ or die.

The movie was successful in scaring me into another salvation. I didn't know what that meant, other than they told me all I had to do was ask Jesus into my heart and He would take all my sins away, making my heart "white as snow," and I now got the privilege of going to heaven (and in my mind, never having to get my head chopped off). Each time I saw that movie, or went to camp, I figured my heart was certainly black again from all my sins, so I would ask Him again and again to forgive me and "save me."

When I was twelve, my best friend told me about the Holy Spirit and how asking the Holy Spirit to fill me would give me more power to withstand the constant pressure of wanting to sin. I went with her to her church and asked the pastor to pray for me for the Holy Spirit to come fill me up, again not understanding what it meant, but I believed it and decided this was the last time I would ever have to ask God to "save me."

I spent the next several years trying to grow as a child of God, yet not finding a good church where they taught me how, or having anyone to walk with me and teach me. I was simply not learning how to have a deep relationship with my Lord. I was never a bad or promiscuous girl, yet I dated many boys just wanting male companionship. I always had this moral compass in me wanting to do what's right, but I cannot say I didn't do some unwise things. I never smoked or did drugs, but I must confess I did fake it a few times so I wouldn't have to explain why I didn't.

More Than Friends

When I was 17 and just getting out of my junior year in high school, I met a young man of 21. I was invited by a friend to visit a youth group where she introduced me to a tall, handsome man named Mike Lynch. I felt something in my heart immediately, but not the usual teenage crush. I did feel that someday we would be more than friends. I began attending this youth group, even though I didn't like the pastor. At the time I didn't know people had spiritual gifts or even that there was a gift of discernment, which I have. I always just thought everyone could tell when someone was lying or cheating. I found out many years later some unspeakable things this man was doing to the youth who were trusted to his care. A story I do not need to get into. I believe I was attending this youth group because I knew God had something for Mike and me.

That summer the youth went on a three-week ministry tour and Mike drove the bus. We did mime and improvisational skits in Colorado and California. Mike was dating someone at the time and she came and sat by me one day on the bus. She said, "I know someday you and Mike will be a couple, but God hasn't told us to break up yet." The statement seemed a little strange to me, yet I knew the part about Mike and me was true. They did break up on that trip and Mike asked me for a date when we returned home. The night before our first date, I dreamt that we were married with three children. Our first date was the Minnesota State Fair, which is an important event in Minnesota and surrounding states. He held my hand on that date, which I thought was way too intimate, and later kissed me on the cheek. I told my sister that night that I would not date him again, which I didn't for one month.

Mike and I began with a friendship and it wasn't long before we realized that we belonged together and God had a plan for our lives. He was my dream gentleman, he was good looking and good to me; it helped that he brought me a gift almost every time he came to see me. We dated throughout my whole senior year, which included going to prom. We became engaged five months after my graduation and were married 10 months later on September 10, 1983.

Mike and I had a very hard first year of marriage. Mike lost his job, he was very ill for weeks with no diagnoses as to what was wrong, I became pregnant, and we had a triple rollover car crash while I was pregnant. Some people from the church we belonged to at the time believed you must be in sin to have such devastating things all happening at once, so we felt very condemned.

While recovering from his illness and the car crash, Mike's parents requested we come visit them in Georgia. We did, not knowing his dad was going to set up an interview for Mike with a company selling industrial machinery. He interviewed and I knew God was moving us, so I went home and packed all our things a week before we got the call saying they would like to hire him.

Five months pregnant, I left my family in Minnesota and moved to Georgia to begin my own family. Four months later our beautiful son, Michael Patrick Lynch, Jr. was born. Mike had a good job, was making more money than we had ever dreamed of and our life was good. Two years later we bought a home and decided it was time to have another child. We welcomed Rachael Kristen on July 7, 1987.

Not Always An Honest Man

We were attending a large church and after a few years we began leading a young marrieds care group. We had many friends, yet we were slightly unhappy with our church because we wanted to be involved with helping and serving people. Mike especially wanted this. This church was very large and the paid staff did most things. Today that church has many outreach programs, but at that time there were none.

During those years I thought things were good and I would have claimed that we both loved God and each other very much; however, I began to discover that Mike was not always an honest man. In fact, there were many lies, mostly empty ones, just to avoid answering my questions and I usually overlooked them. I, myself, was still a "good" Christian, or so I thought, but there was no depth of relationship with the Lord.

It was six years before we decided to have another child. I was five months pregnant, and while putting in a video for my son, I found a dirty video in our VCR. I felt a little ill as I pondered where this might have come from. I thought, "Surely this must be the babysitters," which disturbed me as they were in their 70s and like grandparents to my children. I didn't want to believe it, yet it seemed better than the alternative of it being my husband's. I called Mike and after a moment's pause, he confessed it was his. We set up a counseling meeting and I discovered that Mike had been secretly addicted to pornography for many years. This was a painful discovery, especially during pregnancy when you already feel unattractive enough. I had been feeling as if something was quietly destroying our relationship, but I didn't know what or why until that time. Mike immediately agreed to attend counseling, yet after a couple visits he said he was free. I was naïve when it came to addictions. I learned over the next several months, through much study, that pornography is just as addictive as any drug out there. They say it releases the same endorphins, therefore, is just as dangerous and addictive.

As a child I never saw much love displayed anywhere. I knew my mom loved me, but she wasn't able to be around much because my parents were divorced and Mom had to work two jobs most of the time to provide for us five kids and pay the mortgage without any help from our father.

It's All About Me!

Because I had to listen many times to abuses of my father against my mother and brother and emotional abuses toward us all, I had put up my protective walls and vowed that no man would ever hurt me like that. I decided, at a young age, that I would have the perfect marriage and family. As a Christian I figured the way to do this was to point out Mike's faults when I saw them. I tried, unconsciously of course, to be his Holy Spirit, pointing out everything he needed to change to make my world perfect.

I wanted everyone to love me and make me feel good about myself, but I never felt the need to love others and make them feel good, least of all my own man. I was so insecure; as most of you know, insecure people are self-centered. When we are walking in our self-centered world or soulish realm, we act the opposite of what our spiritual gifts are. My gift of discernment, when walking in the soulish realm, turned into judgment. I judged everyone around me, but couldn't see the massive log in my own eye. In my marriage I thought I needed to change Mike, not myself, so I could be happy.

After I became aware of the pornography, I began to kneel beside my bed and ask God to make Mike a godly man. One time I heard the Lord reply, "WHO IS MORE IMPORTANT TO YOU, MIKE OR ME?" I knew the right answer to that, "You God," but I knew in my heart that I had put Mike first. Not that I loved him more, I didn't know how, but I sought his love and attention more than I sought my God. I looked to Mike to fix a break in my heart from childhood that only God could fix.

It's Going To Hurt!

About a year later, again kneeling at my bed, I again asked God to make Mike a godly man. This time I clearly heard Him say "I WILL, BUT IT IS GOING TO HURT." I loved those first two words, but those last six words hung in my mind for months, wondering what was going to happen next. Mike had already done many things that had hurt me in the past, but nothing prepared me for what came next. God began to lead me to Psalm 28: 6, **"Blessed be the Lord, for He has heard my supplication. The Lord is my strength and my shield, my heart trusts in Him and I am helped."**

Several months went by and our third child, Janell, turned two. I had been noticing that my once very kind husband, who always brought me home gifts, and who frequently said sweet things to me, was not doing these things anymore. I knew this wasn't good, but I didn't know what the problem was. About a week after Janell's second birthday, Mike was in Dallas on a business trip. He hadn't been dealing with pornography in two years, but be aware that when you close a door to one sin, Satan will try to find a window to sneak in. For Mike this happened to be at work in the form of a seductive woman who was able to draw Mike in with things I had failed at, such as compliments, which most men thrive on.

On this business trip I became aware that he may be interested in someone and asked him point blank on the phone. He admitted he was. As a wife, this is the most devastating thing you can ever hear and my heart shattered instantly!

I knew I had to ask him to move out of our house when he came home, although I kept hoping by some miracle it would not have to happen. My hope was that he would say he still loved me and we could work it out. But, he didn't love me and he didn't want to work it out. When I got off the phone with him, God directed me to that verse in Psalms again, **"Blessed be the Lord for He has heard my supplication, the Lord is my strength and my shield, my heart trusts in Him and I am helped."** His promise of "I will make him a godly man, but it's going to hurt" came to me. I knew this was it and I knew there was no easy way out. I was going to have to choose to trust God to be my strength through this.

The next day after that phone call, he returned home and we went to see our pastor. Mike had been counseling with this pastor for a year, every Wednesday. This man pastored a church of many thousands, but he took the time to meet with Mike each week. Mike lied to him week after week for a year telling him everything was great, until that day. The pastor, after speaking with Mike first, had lost hope and proceeded to tell me when I was alone with him that I was a strong woman and could make it through a divorce. I looked him straight in the eyes and said, "That is not what God told me." He told me Mike would be a godly man; therefore, my marriage will be restored!!

Everything In Me Wanting To Scream

I remember when I was in sixth grade we had to do an art project. The teacher asked us to draw what we wanted most to be when we grew up. All I wanted to be was a wife and mother and to have a happy family, so that's what I drew and that continued to be my dream. That day, after leaving our pastor, I realized my dream was dead. The thing I wanted most in life was no longer possible, there would be no "happily ever after" for me. The hardest thing I've ever done was to watch my husband pack his things that day and walk out our door. Everything in me wanting to scream, "I'll do anything, please don't leave!" But in my deepest despair, I knew God must do His perfect work. My lifelong favorite Bible verse is **Romans 8:28, "God works all things together for good for those who love Him and are called according to His purpose."** I had a promise, now I must trust God to fulfill that promise and work it all for good.

I didn't understand at the time that God allowed my dream to die because it was dysfunctional. I needed my deepest desire to be for Christ, not a perfect husband or the perfect family. God was about to have His way in me. I had always desired to be a godly woman, but didn't have a clue how far from it I was. I thought that because I had been a Spirit-filled Christian since the age of 12, that I was a mature Christian. Little did I know my journey to maturity had only just begun.

Mike moved out and so began a six-month spiritual battle that didn't stop for a moment. I went into this not knowing much about prayer or how to pray intercessory prayers. I was suddenly thrust into a battle I had no clue how to fight. Prayer is the first line of defense, yet the enemy must be defeated in our heart and mind before we can begin to battle in prayer. One day, a few weeks after Mike left, I was walking around the block while visiting my family in Minnesota and I felt I needed to be alone and pray.

The enemy was continually discouraging me, which was an easy job as I was getting little sleep because of stress. He loves to prey on the weak. Suddenly I got very angry at the devil; I stopped in my tracks, stomped my foot to the ground and said to him, "ENOUGH! I WILL NOT LET YOU WIN! YOU WILL NOT HAVE MY MARRIAGE AND MY FAMILY! GOD PROMISED ME AND I WILL FIGHT AND NOT STOP UNTIL MY MARRIAGE AND FAMILY ARE RESTORED!!!"

In our trials we have a choice: focus on how difficult it is, complain, feel sorry for ourselves and be defeated, or decide that we will seek out what God is working out for our good and focus on what He is trying to change in **us** through the trial. Once we decide to let God have His way, we must decide to never, never look back, but to fight however we must, to draw near to God and see His work to completion. That day I defeated the enemy in my heart and mind and decided that no matter what, I was going to fight for my promise!

I had been told by many what a jerk Mike was, that I didn't deserve this and to seek a divorce, which I could have done. Or I could lay myself before the Lord and say, "I trust You to deal with Mike. Now do what you need to do in me Lord." This is what I chose to do because I did not want to get in the way of His plan. I began to ask God to teach me how to pray. My gift is not intercession, but during this time He taught me how to intercede for myself, my husband, and my family. Strange things would happen, such as: I would feel a tug in my spirit pulling me into my prayer room when God wanted me to pray. I would begin weeping in the Spirit, learning that this was also intercession. I would ask the spirit to pray through me and spent many hours weeping and praying in the spirit, yet also many very simple, specific prayers.

It was interesting later to discover how God had answered some of those prayers. I remember a couple times praying a shield around Mike that would keep women from being attracted to him. I knew he was going to bars for attention. He was 6 feet 2 inches, 220 pounds, and a very good-looking man. He told me later he would go to bars and could not figure out why not one woman would even speak to him. I told him why. I want to encourage you that prayer is not difficult. When I say I fought in prayer it was mostly simple prayers. God doesn't want our religious garble; He wants honest, simple prayers. He wants a relationship with you. Jesus was becoming not just my Lord, but also my most trustworthy friend.

Still About Me, Yet A Different Me

For six months I learned to depend more on God each day, daily waking up and making my choice to continue in my fight for His promise and for my spiritual freedom. I knew that my marriage, not to mention my own life, could never be restored without me changing drastically. I also knew I could live and be happy without Mike, but, never without Jesus.

I began to ask God to show me my faults, which I knew kept me distant from Him. He very kindly began to slowly walk me through all the hurts that had caused me to be so self-focused and dysfunctional with others in my relationships. I began to forgive those who had wounded me so greatly in my childhood. With every wound or offense we receive as a child we unconsciously gain a little layer of hardness on our heart trying to protect our hearts from future hurts. These layers soon build a tough crust and over the years we become insensitive to others and unable to love.

As I became aware of wounds and forgave, I also began to see how I had wounded others, especially Mike, over the years. I went to Mike several times during our separation to ask for forgiveness as I would recognize where I had wounded him. I do want you to understand that neither I nor Mike ever excused what he did. He made his choice to sin, yet I knew I had my part in this marriage failure. As I submitted to God, He walked me through one personality defect at a time and still is. As I forgave others and myself, my hard heart began to soften and I began to become more sensitive and able to care for others.

Back to our pastor. Mike had told me during our separation, the reason he lied to him week after week was that he felt he would never understand as he was a pastor's son and now a pastor. We had casually known him for many years and he never seemed to have a sin in his life. Mike felt his was too ugly and felt this man could not help him. He was a godly man, but because of what he said to me about getting through a divorce, I knew I needed to find a church where the pastor would believe with me for the restoration of my family.

Simple Things Show You Care

I began to pray for someone who had been there, done that, knowing Mike would eventually need someone when he decided to step back into God's will. I also began to pray for a new church. The fact was that when this news broke in our Sunday school class, we lost nearly every friend we had in an instant. You see, these folks didn't have a clue how to respond, so they turned the other way and ignored it. Only two couples stayed in touch with me to make sure I was okay. A few tried to convict Mike by telling him what he was losing, but in the long run there was only one friend who loved Mike through his sin and never condemned him. I don't blame those people because I may have reacted the same way if I hadn't gone through it.

My friends, if you know someone is hurting, please don't turn the other way, afraid of what to say. It meant more to me than I could ever tell you when someone cared enough to just check on me or invite me and the kids over for dinner, ministering to us by just caring, and it didn't matter what they said. Simple things show you care. One of my biggest blessings was when a neighbor woman, who was a Christian, came to my house and asked if there was anything she could do for me. I told her I wasn't sleeping well and asked if she would read the Bible to me as I rested. I climbed onto my bed and this sweet woman, named Adrian, read to me until I fell asleep.

Not A Sparrow Falls To The Ground Apart From God's Will

I have a story I must share now. A few years prior to this, the kids and I went with my mother back to Minnesota to stay for a couple weeks. On the way we stopped at a gas station and the kids let our little family pet Dachshund, named Ginny, out to do her business. I got back to the car and asked the kids if she was in the car. "She's in her blanket," they replied. An hour and a half later we discovered we hadn't seen her. Everyone went into a panic. I found the number to the station and called them. They said no one had left a dog. So I then called the police in that city, not knowing what else to do.

Then I heard God tell me to read Matthew 10:29, **"Are not two sparrows sold for a copper coin? And not one of them falls to the ground apart from your Father's will."** I read it to the kids and told them "We must trust that it is God's will for some unforeseen reason." Mike put ads in the paper in the city where she became lost, plus she had our name, address and phone number on her tag. We thought surely we would hear something. We even stopped at that station on the way home and they said that someone did leave a dog, but it was not that breed and it was not a female.

Our precious children began to pray every night, "God, would You take care of Ginny, and please bring her home safe." They did this for three months and we finally said to them that Ginny is not coming home, so we can stop praying for her now. Those poor kids cried themselves to sleep that night. The very next night as we kneeled at the bed to pray we heard, "God would you take care of Ginny and please bring her home safe?" Mike and I literally rolled our eyes at each other thinking they didn't hear us too well.

Thank God for children's faith. Within five days a woman called and to make a long story short, her husband worked at that gas station, took our dog home telling his wife he found her and they were going to call her "Ginny." Three months later they were getting a divorce and she found the dog tag in a box of his things. Losing a dog when she was young, she felt compelled to call, even though she fell in love with Ginny. Now, a few years later, I realized why our dog was lost at that time, then found. God knew that these hurting kids and I would one day need something to help them believe through this time.

Every time they would feel sad and doubt, I would say to them, "Remember what God did with Ginny? That's what He's going to do with Daddy." It built their faith every time. Just a few days after Mike left, knowing I would have to keep their faith up, I had them make a banner that said, "WELCOME HOME DADDY!" I told them God promised, so we must be ready for the party when it happens. We tucked it away and waited.

I cannot begin to tell you all the lessons God taught me during this time:

- Peace in a storm
- Patience
- Transformation of my mind by controlling my thoughts
- Forgiveness, others and myself
- Love, others and myself, but most important, God's love for me
- Controlling my tongue
- Not to judge, because after all, I have sinned so many times myself
- Humility and compassion

Each of these fruits, which I am not perfect at yet, came with a prayer, a painful lesson, and my submission to repent and make a study of growing in each fruit. This was not intentional, in fact, I didn't even realize it was happening until I looked back in my journal and noticed the progression of growth that coincided with the verses I was studying at the time.

I would run on faith for days, and then discouragement would come. I would pray for encouragement and God was always faithful to speak a verse to me or have someone give me a call with a word. One day, while praying with a friend, I was extremely discouraged and wanting to give up. I told her, "I NEED TO HEAR FROM GOD."

This friend who was very prophetic, had a word from God: "I HAVE ALREADY TOLD YOU EVERYTHING YOU NEED TO KNOW. TRUST ME WITH EVERY FIBER OF YOUR BEING. YOU WILL SEE THINGS COME TO PASS THAT YOU DON'T EVEN REMEMBER PRAYING FOR. THE END IS IN SIGHT." Sometimes it is so simple and we just complicate it. From the very beginning He said to me simply, "TRUST ME, AND KEEP STANDING." In my moments of discouragement when I would say, "I don't know what else to do," I would hear Him say, "WHAT HAVE I TOLD YOU TO DO?" The answer was to trust Him and keep standing.

I kept going back to that verse in Psalms, **"Blessed be the Lord for He has heard my supplication. The Lord is my strength and my shield, my heart trusts in Him and I am helped. Therefore, my heart greatly rejoices and with my song I will praise Him."**

Blood And Fire – The Release Is About To Come!

This same prophetic friend called me one day and asked me to visit a church with her, so I did. My church was charismatic, but I had not been to one where the new revival fire was going on. I was a little disturbed by what was going on. The woman in front of me was worshipping by crouching up and down over and over with her arms up and she was shaking all over. I turned to my friend and said, "That woman is going home with a headache and a hemorrhoid." I went home vowing never to go to a certain church denomination again.

My friend invited me to go to a downtown ministry church with her the next day. It was a Saturday and she said they have church on Saturday, and then all go out to the projects and feed the poor. This appealed to me so I went with her. We pulled into the driveway of this run down warehouse, right in middle of the projects. It was the most poor, crime ridden, violent area of Atlanta. I walked in the door, looked up at the pastor and felt the Lord say to me, "This is your new church, and that is the man you have been praying for."

During worship I looked on the wall, which had huge banner on it stating that this church was the same denomination I had vowed to never attend again. I thought, "Oh man, I was loving this church and now I can't come because I had made that vow."

After the service I went to the pastor for prayer. He had a lady with beautiful, long, blond hair come to me and lay her hand on my heart. She said to me, "Your heart has been crushed. God is going to restore the pieces." She said she saw me going up a mountain and I was almost to the top. "Hold on," she said, "the release is about to come." Praise God for His continued encouragement!! Incidentally, the pastor did not remember this woman and I never saw her again.

I forgot all about my vow and brought my kids to that church the next day. Everyone at that church remembers my first time because of what I wore. This was a street ministry church, all there were casual. While I, coming from a typical southern church, wore my pretty lace dress and high heels. Never again did I dress like that to go to church. The kids and I loved this church with the cult-sounding name of BLOOD-N-FIRE. Not only could we wear jeans, but also we got to serve the poor, which is something Mike and I had wanted to be part of for years.

The kids began to tell Mike about the pastor wearing blue jeans, Harley boots and riding his Harley right into the church. Plus, they had an incredible band. Mike loved motorcycles and He was slightly curious, but was having too much fun to care and enjoyed having no responsibility.

I began to have joy for the first time since our separation. God ministered to me greatly through the pastor and others at the church. They believed me about what God said and began to pray for our marriage. I would tell them of Mike's talents and the things he would love to do after he started to come with me. I told them Mike had run sound before and would be a great salesman for the T-shirt booth.

Righteous Manipulation

About a month went by and it was our 12th wedding anniversary. For some unknown reason, we decided to go out for dinner together. I had no idea he had full intention of destroying all my hope. I never went to Mike during our separation and asked him to move home or pled my love to him. Twice in six months I told him that I believed God was going to restore our marriage and I still loved him because I chose to.

That day, Sept 10, 1995, as the waitress was putting the food on the table, Mike told me he wanted a divorce. Needless to say, I didn't eat a bite. I went home, again, heartbroken. I called my new pastor and told him what happened. He asked me if Mike would come and see him. I told him, "No, but let me fast and pray for 24 hours, then ask him."

I did that, and after the 24 hours I called Mike and asked him if he would agree to the meeting. I must tell you that we had been to three different marriage counselors, paid and volunteer. None could pull anything out of Mike, so when I asked him to go see another person he responded with, "What is he going to say that the others haven't already said."

Even though I was free of that old, manipulative (spirit) character in me, I figured I would try a little righteous manipulation. I told him if he would go see my new pastor just once, I would sign his divorce papers. Well that worked like a charm. I trusted God's word to me when He let me know that that pastor was the man I had been praying for, that had been there and done that. I knew if I could get Mike there that God would take over.

A few days later I met Mike at the warehouse. As we stood waiting for Pastor David VanCronkhite, Mike asked me again, "What's he going to say? I don't want another counselor." I just said that I didn't know, and that he was the one who asked if he (Mike) would come.

David arrived and introduced himself as he wrapped his arms around Mike, which Mike didn't appreciate too much. We went into his office, which was not a pretty sight, in that old warehouse. David crossed his Harley boots and said to Mike, "I don't want to counsel you. I just want to walk with you a ways if you'll let me." I felt the Holy Spirit's presence. He asked Mike to kick his heels in and stop the train of thought toward divorce for a while. He asked him to stop listening to anything but Christian music, and read one chapter of Acts per day for one week and see what it did to his mind.

Mike had been completely taken in by country music. To this day he partially blames that music for his downfall and refuses to listen to secular music because of the influence it can have on the mind.

Mike was shocked at the difference it immediately made on him. He was at the house at 6:30 A.M the next day digging through his stuff to find his Bible. This was the beginning process, but for three more months I battled. Mike continued to see David, but I knew nothing. The thoughts were hard to control at times still hearing, "Give up," and fighting back with "But God said."

One day Mike came over so we could take the kids school shopping. We went to eat, came home, and I felt as if God wanted me to let Mike know that I knew what he had done and to forgive him. He had never confessed an affair to me, just feelings. God revealed to me the truth: that he had been in an affair for a year and a half. I told Mike this and said that I forgave him. I saw a couple tears as he said, "I don't know how you can, because I can't forgive myself."

To be honest, if someone had asked me a year earlier what I would do if my husband had an affair, I would have stated emphatically that I would leave him! But my God orchestrated things so well with warnings and grace that I responded accordingly, desperately wanting His will over mine.

Mike was coming over a lot now. Many people kept telling me not to let him have his cake and eat it to, but God said to love and serve him, and how could I do that if he wasn't over. I kept it pure. I hadn't been much of a servant to Mike in our marriage. I wanted him to be a servant, not me, but I was seeking to change my old ways and I needed to show Mike love through service.

To you ladies reading this, it's OK, ladies, to serve our man. We are commanded in Ephesians 5:22 to submit to our husbands as unto the Lord. AS UNTO THE LORD! How many of us would treat our Lord the way we do our husbands at times. I know if God were in my home, I WOULD serve Him, so I should serve my husband as well. Most of us instead of respecting and honoring our men, we let words come out our mouths that hammer a little piece of their manhood away from them with our disapproving words, and we never even bat an eyelash. Then we control, manipulate, and blame them for the problems in our marriage.

Society teaches us through many avenues that we have equal rights and yes, we do, legally, but it is a privilege to be a woman. The word says we are the "weaker vessel." In Greek, *weaker* means simply, "not as strong." *Vessel* means "as contributing to the usefulness of." Men are to be the strong pillar and we are the support they need to hold them up. We were created to have someone to lean on. Men are commanded to

LOVE their wives, and most men want to take care of their woman, and they NEED to be needed. It's we women who won't let them lead as God intended them to.

I know there are tough situations out there and some men don't want to walk out who they are supposed to be. But as far as being in a godly marriage, at times we must trust God as we walk out our command to submit and respect, not by letting him walk all over us and we just roll over and take it, but to trust him, respect his opinions, and allow him to be the leader in the home. As we do this, he is being built up as a man and can then love us as Christ loves the church.

There is so much more that could be included here, and please don't read too much into what I am saying. I want you to think about how we, and society, have bought into the lie that to be equal we must be just as strong and capable as men in all areas. It's OK to be a woman and to lean on your man. I have, and am still learning to love and to serve.

One day, a couple weeks later, I was again looking to God for encouragement. I told Him I was scared because I didn't FEEL much love for Mike. I was hurting too much and I needed encouragement again. What a patient God we serve! About ten minutes later, Mike walked in the door. He had spilled coffee on himself on his way to work and since I had been offering to clean his car, it looked like a great opportunity to him, because there was now coffee on the seats. He kept staring at me, then he left, came back in, gave me a hug and said I was beautiful.

I stood in shock for a minute or so. Considering I hadn't heard a nice word from him in many months, I took that as encouragement. Still the battle went on. I didn't realize until later that there was a battle going on within Mike also. He didn't love me; in fact, he had hated me for quite some time, to the point of wishing me dead. He didn't know how to do what was right when his feelings were in the way. He had heard me talk about love being a choice, and it wasn't one he was ready to make.

Mike began to make some effort to do things with me. One day he asked me to go for a drive to the mountains. We lived in Georgia and it was only about an hour to the foothills. We had a great day, but then he left at night with no word or sign that he was ready to come home. I made sure God knew, and Mike knew, that I didn't want him half home. Not until he was 100 percent sure he was going to live for God first, then family.

He was still going to see my pastor and I didn't have a clue what they talked about. It was very difficult to deal with. One day Mike said to me that he was ready to begin counseling with me, but, David had said he needed to get honest with me and share something first, and he was ready. He came over that evening to share whatever it was. He was unable to speak it, so I told him, "I don't want to see your face in this house again or speak to you until you are ready to commit 100 percent," and he walked out the door. Because I knew it was the right time to say this was the only reason I was so harsh.

God Is The God Of Suddenlies

We didn't speak for five days. It was the fifth day and I was completely grieved. The enemy was giving me all kinds of negative thoughts and I entertained them for a while. I felt as if I was surrounded by the enemy. I went to my faithful Father again, asking Him what to do. Again, He said, "I have told you from the beginning to KEEP STANDING AND TRUST ME." At that moment I was led to Psalm 3:1, 2, 3: **"OH LORD, HOW MANY OF MY FOES RISE UP AGAINST ME SAYING GOD WILL NOT DELIVER ME! BUT YOU OH LORD, ARE A SHIELD AROUND ME. YOU BESTOW GLORY ON ME AND LIFT UP MY HEAD."** I said to Him, "I WILL keep trusting!" and I kneeled down and repented for my negative feelings.

I repented for emotionally clinging to Mike and for thinking that I could do anything about my situation. At last I could completely lay Mike down at His feet. Feeling complete freedom and joy, I jumped up and down and danced around my house in a victory dance. I continued in this for quite awhile. It was as if the Lord heard this and said, "Finally, she has given it completely to me. Angels, go minister to her and send her husband home." About an hour later the phone rang. It was Mike saying he wanted to come home! Wow! God is a God of suddenness.

Like Joseph, in prison for years and then one day, suddenly, someone remembers him, he's released, and before the day is over he's second in charge of Egypt. That day, suddenly, what I had been praying about for years and in prayer, battling, for six months, all the grief, it was accomplished. Suddenly Mike was saying, "I want to come home." I got off the phone and went right back to my praising and dancing.

Again, remembering my Psalms verse: **"Blessed be the Lord for He has heard my supplication. The Lord is my strength and my shield, my heart trusts in Him and I am helped. Therefore my heart greatly rejoices and with my song I will praise Him."** Now I was definitely praising Him. Shortly after this the kids came home and we had a celebration dance.

The next day we were in for counseling before he moved back home. He confessed all, but I had already forgiven all and made that clear to him again. David told Mike he felt that they would someday be working together, full-time, which seemed impossible to Mike as that would mean full-time missions. Mike's appearance – his countenance – changed instantly. Not his clothing or hair, but many saw the change in his eyes. That evening the kids hung their banner and we had a welcome home party.

Restoration

Mike and I began the difficult, but joyful walk of restoration. We were now all attending BNF (Blood-N-Fire) and Mike jumped right in with serving the poor on the streets. We were doing several outreaches a week, going out with the band and setting up feeding lines. I usually spent my time playing with the kids in the projects while Mike helped with food and whatever needs there were.

Mike's favorite part was the "hug line." We would make the people go through a hug line to get the food. We would all line up and hug them, one by one, tough and mean, inner-city adults, many who had not been hugged in years. Some would bust out in tears by the time they got their food from the love being shown.

Mike was also now helping do the sound and running the T-shirt booth. I had five kids in the projects that I would spend every Saturday with. After we would finish the Saturday outreach and kids' church, I would do something with the five kids. It was different each week.

Slowly and surely our marriage got better and better. Mike and I renewed our wedding vows six months later, as most of them had been broken. Within two years, Mike, at the Lord's calling, quit his full-time job and we became full-time, inner city missionaries. Mike also became an associate pastor at Blood-N-Fire Ministries in Atlanta, Georgia. We began to notice he was gifted at procuring products and foodstuff to give away to the poor.

Five years later God told us to move to Minneapolis, where we co-founded a ministry that began by Mike delivering fresh bread to ministries. It grew to multimillions in value, per year, of food, clothing, medical supplies and such being given away. God eventually had us leave that place, but that was only the beginning of us being used to serve the poor here and abroad for many years now.

As I write, Mike is doing disaster relief work, overseeing the giving away of hundreds of tons of food, cleaning supplies, clothing, building supplies and such things that are needed after a disaster. He has been used to send countless truckloads of food to several countries and states to feed the hungry.

This testimony is not just about a marriage restored. It's about two hard hearts restored. It's about two lives that were completely complacent, asleep in their Christian walk, waking up and finding out what it means to completely turn oneself over to the will of God and walk as children of light. God loved us enough that He allowed a painful situation to jolt me into reality of who He is in my life if I only let Him.

I went on a six-month crash course in spiritual growth. It only just began those many years ago. Still my daily stand is to be more like Jesus and I continue to lay myself before Him each day and ask Him to cleanse me from any ungodly traits left in me. I will continue on a lifelong journey in growth.

Mike and I have counseled many individuals and many couples. It never ceases to amaze us at how few understand how to walk out their proclaimed salvation or how to daily walk in God's will. Unfortunately, most Christians go to church on Sunday and hear a great message that inspires them momentarily. Then they walk the same walk and talk the same talk they did the week before.

If you are not changing every week, you are not maturing in your walk with God. My desire in writing this book is to give some simple revelations and truths in an understandable way to guide those who have just given their life to the Lord, or to those who did it many years ago and haven't quite understood what happened, or how to change and be more like Jesus.

PART TWO:

WHAT IT MEANS
TO BE "BORN AGAIN"
AND HOW TO WALK IT OUT

– 1 –

What Does It Mean
To Be "Born Again" Or "Saved"?

John 3:3-8 Jesus answered Nicodemus and said, **"Most assuredly, I say to you, unless one is born again he cannot see the kingdom of God."** Nicodemus said to Him, **"How can a man be born when he is old? Can he enter a second time into his mother's womb and be born?"** Jesus answered, **"Most assuredly I say to you, unless one is born of water and the Spirit, he cannot enter the Kingdom of God. That which is born of the flesh is flesh, and that which is born of the Spirit is Spirit. Do not marvel that I said to you 'you must be born again.' The wind blows where it wishes and you hear the sound of it, but cannot tell where it comes from and where it goes. So is everyone who is born of the Spirit."**

This profound scripture tells the necessity of being "born again." We CANNOT see the kingdom of God without it. Jesus explains that there is the water birth, meaning the natural birth, that happens when we leave the womb and enter the world. Then there is the "Spirit" birth. Our spirit is that part of us that cannot die, the part that is capable of responding to God. When we are born of water or flesh, our soul, (our mind, will and emotions) comes to the forefront naturally and controls our words and actions throughout our life.

We will act according to how our mind, will, and emotions have been trained to respond and act. They are trained by the events that have surrounded us during our life and upbringing. Our soul naturally reigns dominant over our spirit. When we are born again, our spirit comes alive and comes to the forefront. Just as when a baby comes out of the womb and breathes its first breath of life, when you are born of the spirit you breathe your first spiritual breath.

Let me give an explanation: When God created the earth and all in it, man was the only living being that He breathed his own breath into. Genesis 2:7 says, **"And the Lord God formed man of the dust of the ground, and breathed into his nostrils the breath of life; and man became a living being."** He created Adam from the dust. He was lifeless until God put His mouth over Adam's nostrils and breathed life into him.

When you are born of the Spirit, God breathes his spiritual life into you. Your spirit is immediately *awakened* and you have a new life. At that moment you are re-created in a sinless state, just as Adam was originally created. 2 Corinthians 5:17 says, **"Therefore, if anyone is in Christ, he is a new creation; old things have passed away; behold all things have become new."** For those of you who have been "born again," you may remember the euphoria you felt, as if you had a whole new life, fresh and clean. Well you did and you still do. The old you (your sinful nature) was put to death and you became righteous (in right standing with God) at that moment, through the shed blood of Jesus Christ.

How Am I Born Again/Saved?

1 John 1:9 says, **"If we confess our sins, He is faithful and just to forgive us our sins and to cleanse us from all unrighteousness."** Romans 10:9 says, **"If you confess with your mouth the Lord Jesus and believe in your heart that God raised Him from the dead, you will be saved."** The first scripture states we should admit we are a "sinner" in need of a Savior who can forgive us. The second scripture means that we confess that Jesus is that Savior. We must speak these words with our mouth first as a spoken confession declares and confirms it in our heart. We then must also believe that Jesus was born, died, and rose again to give us this privilege.

That's the simplicity of being "born again." Then the journey begins. For a newborn, breathing life on earth begins the moment they come out of the womb and into the world. In the same way, your Christian walk begins the moment you speak your confession of belief in Jesus Christ. This book is about how to go about growing as a Christian, not just getting into heaven, but living a victorious life while you are here on this earth.

Why Did Jesus Have To Shed His Blood And Die?

I am not going to get into great detail here as it is not the focus of this book, but I know many do not even know the reason Jesus had to shed His blood and die. I, therefore, will try to give some simple understanding of the purpose.

In the Old Testament it was necessary for blood to be shed, through a sacrifice, to atone for one's sin. *Atone* means to make amends for a wrong. Anytime someone sinned an atonement was necessary for them to be clean again. This atonement was done through sacrificing an animal and shedding its blood on an altar. The animal was to be a blemish-free animal in order to be accepted.

Leviticus 17:11 explains why blood was necessary, **"For the life of the flesh is in the blood, and I have given it to you upon the altar to make atonement for your souls; it is the blood that makes atonement for your souls."** So, in order to be in right standing with God, a sacrifice would be necessary every time a sin was committed.

In Isaiah 7:14, Isaiah prophesied the coming of the Son of God: **"Behold, the virgin shall conceive and bear a son, and shall call His** name **Emmanuel**" (which means God with us). Isaiah 52 verses 13-15 and all of chapter 53 is a prophetic word about Jesus Christ, what he would go through, and why. Starting in 53:4, "**Surely He has borne our griefs and carried our sorrows; He was wounded for our transgressions, He was bruised for our iniquities, the chastisement for our peace was upon Him, and by His stripes we are healed. All we like sheep have gone astray; We have turned, everyone to his own way; and the Lord has laid on Him (Jesus) the iniquity of us all....He was led as a lamb to the slaughter.**" These words were given about 700 years before Jesus was born.

Matthew 1:21 says, "**And she** (the virgin) **will bring forth a son, and you shall call His name JESUS, for He will save His people from their sins.**" John the Baptist was born for the purpose of going before Jesus to prepare the way for Him (Luke 1:5-17). John 1:6-7 says, "**There was a man sent from God, whose name was John. This man came for a witness, to bear witness of the light** (Jesus) **that all might believe.**" John proclaimed that the Christ (or Messiah) was coming.

One day, while baptizing people, John saw Jesus coming and stated, "**Behold, the Lamb of God who takes away the sin of the world**" (John 1:29). John proclaimed publicly that Jesus was born for the sole purpose of offering His life as the perfect, spotless and infinite sacrifice for the transgressions of man forever, THE LAMB OF GOD! When Jesus shed His perfect blood, it made atonement for man's sin forever, never again would we, or priests have to kill an animal and drain the blood on an altar to be forgiven.

Hebrews 10:12-14 says, "**But this Man, after He had offered one sacrifice for sins forever, sat down at the right hand of God...For by one offering He has perfected forever those who are being sanctified.**" Through Jesus death, we were made perfect, yet we are being sanctified daily (being made holy) as we make choices to walk in His will for us. I will talk more about that later on.

Suffice all this to say, Jesus was born to be a spot free sacrifice and to shed His blood to be the atonement for our sins once and for all, FOREVER.

2

WHO IS THE HOLY SPIRIT?

In this chapter I will briefly introduce to you who the Holy Spirit is, and the rest of the book will bring more clarity and understanding.

Jesus spoke to a woman in John 4:14 saying, **"But whoever drinks of the water that I shall give him will never thirst, but the water that I shall give him will become in him a fountain of water springing up into everlasting life."** If we look to another passage we find out what this "fountain of water" means. John 7:38 says, **"'He who believes in Me as the scripture has said, out of his heart will flow rivers of living water,' But this He spoke concerning the Spirit, whom those believing in Him would receive, for the Holy Spirit was not yet given, because Jesus was not yet glorified."**

Jesus was letting them know, ahead of time, that a precious gift was coming that would give them continuous channels of refreshment. John the Baptist told the people in John 1:8, **"I indeed baptize you with water, but He will baptize you with the Holy Spirit."** Jesus reiterated this statement in Acts 1:8. He said, **"You shall receive power when the Holy Spirit has come upon you and you shall be witnesses unto me..."** John 14:15-16 says, **"If you love Me, keep My commandments. And I will pray to the Father, and He will give you another helper, that He may abide with you forever."** Verse 26 says, **"...the Helper, the Holy Spirit, whom the Father will send in My name, He will teach you all things and bring to your remembrance all things that I said to you."**

The Holy Spirit Gives Us Continuous Guidance

Jesus tells us that it is to our advantage for Him to go away (back to heaven) because if He does not go away the Holy Spirit cannot come and dwell in us (John 16:5-14). Jesus tells us that it will be the Holy Spirit that gives us power, and guides us into all truth (Act 1:8). While Jesus walked the earth He could be with people, but He was not in them. The Holy Spirit (God in spirit form) dwells in us, thereby, giving us continuous guidance into all truth (John 16:13).

In my testimony, I told that I asked a pastor to lay hands on me, as they did in Acts 19:6, and pray for the Holy Spirit to fill me. I never again doubted my salvation after that because the Spirit of truth now abides in me. Some people believe you must ask for the infilling of the Holy Spirit; some believe it just comes with salvation. I personally believe it comes with salvation, but as in my case, the laying on of hands just activated my faith in the power that comes with the Holy Spirit. If you need a little activation prayer, you can lay your own hands on yourself and ask God for the Holy Spirit to come alive in you in power and truth.

Jesus Himself did not begin His ministry until He was anointed by the Holy Spirit of God. When He was baptized by John the Baptist, Mathew 3:16 says, **"When He had been baptized, Jesus came up immediately from the water, and behold, the heavens were opened to Him and He saw the Spirit of God [the Holy Spirit] descending like a dove and alighting upon Him."** That was the moment He received the anointing, and it was the beginning of His Ministry here on earth. Up to that point He had not done any miracles nor had He begun to teach. Jesus was the first to receive the infilling of the Holy Spirit, and according to John 16:7, no one else could receive this gift until Jesus went away.

John 16:7 says, **"Nevertheless I tell you the truth, it is to your advantage that I go away; for if I do not go away, the Helper will not come to you; but if I depart I will send Him to you."**

Now all we need to do is ask and believe!

3

NOW WHAT?

Once you are "born again," you should immediately plug into a church that teaches God's whole word (the Bible) as absolute truth. Pray and ask God to lead you to this church, and then search until God gives you a peace about it. Just as a newborn needs someone to nurture and feed them, you not only need a good church, but also it would be of great benefit for you to have spiritually mature people beside you to walk with, learn from, and be accountable to. Again, pray and ask God to bring you a few trustworthy, mature people. However, neither they nor the church are responsible for your growth, only you are.

The following chapters will assist you in learning how to grow, or if you have been led off the path after being a Christian for awhile, how to wake up and get back on track.

You Have Purpose

When I was "born again," as a young person, I prayed a prayer of salvation because I was told I needed to in order to get into heaven. Heaven was my purpose for praying for salvation. I did not want to go to hell. I wanted to live forever in glory, (and not worry about my head on the chopping block). I never considered at that time, that God had a purpose for me while I lived on earth.

Unfortunately, too many "believers" are content with the fact that they got their ticket into Heaven and they do not make it a priority to mature in their walk with God, learning to love Him more and receiving His love in order to know their purpose. The truth is that we all have great purpose here and now. That purpose is to love God along with loving people. In Mathew 22:37-41, after being asked what the greatest commandment is, Jesus replied, **"You shall love the Lord your God with all your heart, with all your soul, and with all your mind. This is the first and great commandment, and the second is like it, You shall love your neighbor as yourself. On these two commandments hang all the law."** ALL THE LAW!! Whoa, Jesus is saying if we can follow just those two commandments, we are completely in God's will and need not worry about the others, as they are all summed up in the two.

If we really love God, we will desire to know Him, be like Him, and make Him known to others, allowing Him to love them through us. I decided years ago, while doing disaster relief, that my motto for life will be: "LOVE GOD, LOVE PEOPLE!" That is those two all-important commandments summed up in four words. That is what Jesus did and that is our mission as Christians; it is what we are called to do. It is what makes Christianity so special and set apart from all other religions, because it is all about LOVE! It is also what makes it so misunderstood, because so few understand their call to LOVE!

We Cannot Love Our Neighbor If We Don't Love Ourselves

Once we give our life to the Lord, find a church and, hopefully, have support around us, it is time to allow Him to rid us of characteristics that are not like His. The two most precious things I gained during my separation from my husband was the ability to love God and myself. If those two areas of our life are not healthy, we cannot love at all. We cannot love our neighbor as ourselves if we don't love ourselves, and it is difficult to love ourselves when we are full of unlovely issues.

If we earnestly desire to be like Christ, He will pave the way for us each day. Along the way we will recognize and deal with the "unlovely issues" in our life, and this will cause us to love God and ourselves more, therefore, making us capable of loving others. But, we must hear His direction and walk accordingly. We do not need to be rid of ungodly characteristics before we reach out and love others. In fact, as we step out in obedience and love others, it opens the door for healing in us. God does special things in our heart as we choose to love others.

Agape Love Always Seeks The Highest Good Of The Other Person

Agape love is God's kind of love. It is defined in Wikipedia as divine, unconditional, self-sacrificing, active, voluntary, and thoughtful love. Agape love **always seeks the highest good of the other person**. It is to love someone by choice, not emotion, such as the unconditional love God has for us. It is to love no matter what they do or say and love them intentionally through it all! This kind of love doesn't come easy, but through the Holy Spirit living in us we are able to love even the most unlovely people.

Romans 5:5 says, **"The love of God has been poured out in our hearts by the Holy Spirit who was given to us."** If His love is poured into us, we certainly are able to love like Him. I have watched many lives completely change because someone chose to love that person in an *agape* way. This is the highest and greatest purpose we have! The ultimate goal of this kind of love is to draw them to the One who is LOVE, God their heavenly Father.

This call to love will look different for each person. We are called to love everyone, but times will come when God puts specific people in our lives that He wants us to display His agape love to by choosing to love them and seeking their highest good.

Someone may be called to love a prostitute on the street, or children in Africa, but another may be called to love the wealthy CEO of the company they work for. A young mother may be called to love her next-door neighbor, and her husband is to love his co-workers. Sometimes God will have you show His love to the cashier at a store for just one minute of your life. As we grow and mature as children of God, loving Him and loving people, we will grow more into our destiny. This is what we were born to do, leading more to Him by exampling His love to them through us.

It will take time to mature and learn to love in this way, but God will encourage and guide you every step of the way, if you are willing. It will be an incredible adventure, and life will never be boring as you grow and display His love for His sons and daughters, helping them draw nearer to Him.

Ask Him to put people in your path. Look for them and be ready to intentionally say and do things to make them feel loved.

– 4 –

THE ROAD TO MATURITY

You should know that it won't be long after your salvation that the enemy will be at the doorstep of your mind trying to distract you from your new life. **1 Peter 5:8 says, "Be sober, be vigilant; because your adversary, the Devil, walks about like a roaring lion, seeking whom he may devour. Resist him, steadfast in the faith, knowing that the same sufferings are experienced by your brotherhood in the world."**

The enemy (demonic forces) is sneaky and he knows your weaknesses. He will remind you of them often and will set up situations where you will be confronted with them. However, there's good news! 1 Corinthians 10:13 says, **"No temptation has overtaken you except that which is common to man; but God is faithful, who will not allow you to be tempted beyond which you are able, but with the temptation will also make the way of escape, that you may be able to bear it."**

Be strong in the Lord and know there is not a temptation that is original. God will not allow more than you can bear, and there is always an escape route for you. Remember that you are a "NEW creation," that the old you is dead and only you can bring that old you back to life. The enemy will try to help you raise up that old self and will bring about whatever it takes to distract you from becoming a stronger child of God. Be vigilant in expecting the enemy and resist his distractions, as distractions lead to weakness when temptations come.

What Is A Distraction?

A distraction is anything that becomes priority over knowing God or walking in His will. These are not always bad things. In fact, a lot of times it may be something that must be done, yet it should not keep you from your time with God (i.e. reading the word and talking with Him).

You know better than anyone what your distractions are most likely to be. Think for just a moment... could it be money, or success? Maybe getting a new car or house? Maybe just cleaning the house? It could be a diet or exercise, any sin, or even just a wandering mind. Whatever it is, it becomes an ungodly distraction when it is more of a priority to you than your time with God.

There will always be things that need to be done or things that we love to do. But don't let it keep you from keeping your eyes fixed on the prize, as **1 Corinthians 9:24-27 says, "Do you not know that those who run in a race all run, but one receives the prize. Run in such a way that you may obtain it."** Paul, in this scripture, goes on to say how he disciplines himself and brings his body into subjection so that he will not be disqualified from the race. The race is the road to Christian maturity or godliness. Distractions are what eat up our time and prevent us from that maturity.

Our focus each day should be becoming a bit more like Jesus than we were yesterday. **Joshua 24:15 says, "Choose for yourselves this day whom you will serve."** We make a choice each day to serve God or the things of our world. **Psalm 5:8, "Lead me O Lord, in Your righteousness, because of my enemies make Your way straight."** Pray this verse each day.

If we are to look at the race as a road to maturity and picture it as a very long highway, at the end of the highway, at our destination, it says "GODLINESS," and at the bottom it says, "BORN AGAIN." Imagine you're on the highway heading somewhere, (pretend you don't need gas). The easiest and quickest way to get where you are going is to go straight and don't get off. There will be many off ramps of temptations and distractions on this road.

GPS are great for directions. If you are looking for a place, it will ask you, "Do you want the shortest way or the fastest way?" The highway is always the fastest, and it gives you the time you will arrive. I tend to get more impatient with the GPS on because every time we get off on a ramp (a distraction) for anything, it will add the minutes you took to do whatever you did to the time of arrival. So even though when you first got in the car it said you would be there at 5:30, because of all the stops you now are getting there at 6:15.

This is the same as our highway (road) to Christian maturity. You can stay on the fastest route, the straight line of discipline, and mature more quickly, or you can be distracted by the off ramps and take a little, or a lot longer, depending on how long you linger at each distraction. In life, our distractions can be a minute, a day, a year, or many years. The longer they are, the more weak and feeble a Christian we remain.

Straighten Up And Fly Right

I had a Bible study at my house for a few years. I asked the women one day, "How are you different this week than last week?" They were taken by surprise. One said, "I don't think I am any different this week." If you can't come up with something that has changed, or that God has taught you in the last week, then you have been distracted by the things of life.

Hebrews 12:12-13 says, **"Therefore, strengthen the hands which hang down, and the feeble knees, and make straight paths for your feet, so that what is lame may not be dislocated, but rather healed."** When I read this, for some reason I think of that old song, "Straighten Up and Fly Right!" Just keep your eyes fixed on the goal and do whatever is necessary to get there.

One day I was listening to a TV preacher. He told the story of an astronaut that was on the very first trip to the moon. Because the moon had not been reached before, they weren't quite sure of the course. The astronaut said that in this first trip it was necessary to recalculate their course every ten minutes to get to their destination. Just like that GPS, when I miss my turn it says, "recalculating" and refigures how to get me back on the right route. When we first become a Christian it may be every ten minutes that we have to recalculate and ask ourselves, "Am I on the right track?" As we mature it should become less often that we need to recalculate. Ask yourself often, "Am I different this week than last?" Then, if the answer is "No," if you haven't gained any spiritual wisdom, ask God to help you recognize your distractions and be more disciplined.

THREE ESSENTIALS FOR US TO MATURE

There are three essentials for us to mature: study, prayer, and worship.

1. STUDY

1 Peter 2:2 says, "**As newborn babes, desire the pure milk of the word that you may grow...**" The Word of God is an absolute necessity in your daily life.

A fine truth of why we need the word is in 2 Timothy 3:16: "**All scripture is given by inspiration of God, and is profitable for doctrine, for reproof, for correction, for instruction in righteousness, that the man (woman) of God may be complete, thoroughly equipped for every good work.**"

We must believe that the Holy Bible is not just a book of stories and rules, but it is the absolute and true word of God. "Inspiration of God" means, *God breathed*. We must believe that through the hands of men with pens, God breathed His words onto paper, which were put together to form the Bible. Genesis to Revelation, every book has a purpose. Within this beautiful book are the answers to any problem you may have. Daily study of it equips us for the issues we will face each day.

There are no short cuts to Christian maturity, and it will take discipline, as does anything worthwhile. You may become discouraged at times, but don't give up! If you look for a small revelation from God each day through His word, you will surely find it. James 1:5 says, "**If any of you lacks wisdom, let him ask of God, who gives to all liberally and without reproach.**" Ask for wisdom and expect to learn as you search. It will become the greatest joy of your day.

I remember when I was 18, I went to a seminar and the speaker told us we should commit to the Lord to read a certain amount of the Bible each day, so I did. I committed to God that I would read one chapter per day. If I make a promise, I try my best to keep it. I would come home late some nights after being out with my boyfriend, who is now my husband, and I would always look for the shortest Psalm I could find, just to keep my promise. It became a burden and not a joy to me. Why? Because I wasn't looking to become more like God, or learn more about His ways. I was legalistically reading as fast as I could to keep a foolish promise. I was young and didn't know any better than to do what I was told.

My heart was right when I made the promise, and I really wanted to be a better Christian, but the approach was wrong. It is not wrong to make a commitment, but it should be one with the right purpose. For example, I might make a commitment of 10 minutes a day to search the word for His help in a certain area that I struggle with, such as keeping my peace. I look into the word to see what it says about peace and study a few scriptures accordingly. I look in the concordance for the word *peace* and I find Philippians 4:6-7: **"Be anxious for nothing, but in everything, by prayer and supplication, with thanksgiving, let your requests be known to God; and the peace which surpasses all understanding will guard your hearts and minds through Christ Jesus."**

In that 10 minutes I learned that if take my issues to God in prayer and thanksgiving, His peace will come and guard my heart and mind. Maybe a few days later it's fear, so I now look up fear. Some days it may only be 10 minutes, some days it may be an hour. A commitment can be good, and is usually a necessary discipline, as long as it has a positive growth purpose.

Study For Guidance

Psalms 3:5-6 says, **"Trust in the Lord with all your heart, and lean not on your own understanding; in all your ways acknowledge Him and He shall direct your path."** There are many Christians who are feeling their way around in the dark; their lives are full of stress and strongholds, which prevent them from seeing their way clearly to growth. Eventually they find themselves on a dark path away from Christ that they never intended to go down because they couldn't see clearly what lay ahead on that path until they got there.

Have you ever tried to walk in a strange place or path in the dark? You walk cautiously, with your arms outstretched, feeling to see if the path is safe. Or imagine you're on that highway again. You're in the middle of nowhere and there are no lights on the road or on your car. You would have to pull over and wait until you could see, or great harm, maybe even death, could come to you.

This scripture is telling us that the only way to get clear vision of our path (our road to maturity) is to trust in God. The only way to learn to trust Him is to get to know Him, and the best way to get to know Him is to study His ways. Psalm 119:105 says, **"Your word is a lamp to my feet and a light to my path."** If you are on that dark path and you have a lamp, it will light your feet so you can see if there are any obstacles in the way that you may trip on. But a lamp will not show you what's up ahead.

A light shining on your path is also needed to let you know if what's ahead is safe, so you won't walk off a cliff or step into a lake. Daily study keeps the lamp on your path for right now, but also prepares you for what might be up ahead tomorrow, so you don't veer off the path, or road, into a possible danger zone. Stop and wait for the light. The faster you seek it out, the faster you are on your way safely.

Study To Become Firmly Established

Psalm 1:1-3 says, **"Blessed is the man who walks not in the counsel of the ungodly, nor stands in the path of sinners, nor sits in the seat of the scornful; But his delight is in the law of the LORD, and in His law he meditates day and night. He shall be like a tree planted by the rivers of water, that brings forth its fruit in its season, whose leaf also shall not wither; And whatever he does shall prosper."**

This great scripture promises us that we shall be as strong as a tree near the river when we are not letting the ungodly around us influence the choices we make in our daily life, when our joy comes from searching His word and feeding ourselves from His river. A tree near water gets constant nourishment and therefore grows faster than one not constantly fed. The roots establish themselves and the tree will not waver and fall with the winds that come. Likewise, you will not be falling or stepping off the right path spiritually because you're feeding on wisdom, daily establishing a godly root system.

If you have trouble understanding the Word at first, get a good Bible study from your local Christian bookstore, along with a good concordance. A good study will give you practice on how to find answers in the Bible, and help you to learn to look for the profitable instruction in each and every story. A concordance is a book of words in the Bible and where in the Bible you can find them, such as I mentioned earlier about looking up *peace*. The most effective tool though is to get guidance from the Holy Spirit.

Righteous Anger Or Judgment?

I will give a personal example of how the word can give guidance. There was a time in our lives when we were joined closely with another Christian couple. Without getting into details, they took credit for an event Mike spent months planning. Afterward, they publicly exaggerated the outcome of this event in order to make themselves look good. Our family and friends had worked very hard at this event. I became offended, angry, and stressed about it. For me, it was not about who did it, it was about truth. I was angry that this event was done in the name of the Lord and the truth was not told about the outcome.

During my second sleepless night as I agonized over this situation, the Lord got my attention. He led me to read about David and Saul, specifically where David had Saul in a place where he could have killed him. This great story is found in 1 Samuel 24, and there are many lessons from David's life. If you are not familiar with the story, Saul was king of Israel at this time, but the Lord was displeased with him and had the prophet Samuel anoint David to be the next king while David was just a boy. David became a great warrior and was loved by the people.

Saul, knowing how the people loved David and because he had already been anointed to be the next king, was very jealous and desired greatly to take David's life. David was running from Saul and was hiding in a cave with his men. Saul, while seeking David, along with three thousand of his chosen men, wandered into David's cave alone. David's men told him that the Lord had delivered his enemy into his hands at that moment, but David refused to touch **"the Lord's anointed."** He was able to sneak up and cut off a portion of Saul's robe without Saul being aware of it.

Afterwards David felt very troubled for what he had done to **"the anointed of the Lord."** He went out of the cave and humbly called to Saul, bowing low before him, telling him that the Lord delivered him into his hands and he was urged to kill him, but **"I will not stretch my hand out against the Lord, for he** (Saul) **is the Lords anointed."**

David had every right to be angry as he had done nothing wrong and Saul sought to kill him. David was forced to run for his life and hide in caves, yet he didn't become offended or angry. David said to Saul, **"Let the Lord judge between you and me, and let the Lord avenge me on you, but my hand shall not be against you"** (24:12).

This is the verse that really convicted me. I had made myself judge over the other couple in this situation. I wanted to expose them and let people know what these people had done. I was the only one suffering in my bitterness. That night I gave the situation to God, repenting for my self-righteousness, and I gave the right to judge back to the Lord.

The lesson from God's word that night has not been forgotten; it changed my life. I have had many opportunities to be offended by people since then, and sometimes I go to that place of judgment for a while. But God is always right there to quickly remind me to give it to Him. As I continue to grow in Christ, I usually spend very little time pondering on the wrong things people do and try to focus on what God is teaching me in each situation.

There is an answer in the Bible for everything, you just need to take the time to ask and search.

2. PRAYER

Prayer is also essential to your growth as a child of God. Some may think that to pray you must be in a somber mood, kneel down and fold your hands to talk with God. Prayer is about conversation with God, not an act or position. There may be times when you do need to get on your knees, but the word says we're to pray without ceasing (1 Thessalonians 5:17). That is impossible to do on your knees, but it can be a heart focus all the time.

You can talk with God anytime, anywhere, and in any position. You can talk to Him just as you would a dear friend. Talk about your day, your struggles, your fears, your joys. It is even OK to talk to Him about others (it's not gossip when you're talking to Him). You can talk to Him while driving, shopping, exercising, and even while working. But, there are times that you will need to sit quietly and talk with Him. The reason for quiet is because prayer should be a two-way conversation. As you practice talking to Him in quiet, you will begin to hear His voice speak to you also. This takes time and practice, because you must get your own thoughts out of the way and listen for His voice.

Teach Me To Pray

Our greatest example of prayer is taught by Jesus in Matthew 6:5-15. Verses 5-7 say:

"And when you pray, you shall not be like the hypocrites. For they love to pray standing in the synagogues and on the corners of the streets, that they may be seen by men. Assuredly, I say to you, they have their reward. But you, when you pray, go into your room, and when you have shut your door, pray to your Father who is in the secret place; and your Father who sees in secret will reward you openly. And when you pray, do not use vain repetitions as the heathen do. For they think that they will be heard for their many words."

If we are only praying when people can see or hear us, we are hypocrites and our prayers will never be answered. Your prayers should be as fervent, or more fervent in private than they are in public. We don't need to chant over and over our requests; we should be specific and genuine, making our request known, then trusting Him with the answer. Verse 8 says, **"Therefore do not be like them. For your Father knows the things you have need of before you ask Him. In this manner, therefore, pray."**

In Luke's account of this it says, "His disciples asked him, 'Lord, teach us to pray'"(chapter 11).

Jesus replied, "When you pray, say:

"Our Father in heaven, Hallowed be Your name." Start out telling Him how great He is. Thank Him for all He is, what He has done, and for how much He loves you.

Verse 10: **"Your kingdom come. Your will be done, on earth as it is in heaven."** Let Him know you are submitting yourself to His rule over you and His will for your day.

Verse 11: **"Give us this day our daily bread."** Trust Him and get specific about your needs each day.

Verse 12: **"And forgive us our debts, as we forgive our debtors."** Check your heart daily and specifically forgive those you have issues with, so He can forgive you.

Verse 13: **"And do not lead us into temptation, but deliver us from the evil one."** Ask for wisdom to know how the enemy is distracting you during your day.

"For Yours is the kingdom and the power and the glory forever. Amen." Give Him verbal praise and let Him know that you know who has all the power and deserves all the glory.

Jesus adds this little piece of important information:

Verse 14: "For if you forgive men their trespasses, your heavenly Father will also forgive you. "But if you do not forgive men their trespasses, neither will your Father forgive your trespasses."

This is our guideline for prayer. It is not a prayer to just repeat, but for us to look to as a guide, then we expound and add details according to our own lives, our needs, and our love for Him. We must be specific in our prayers because prayer is much more than just conversation with God. God will do nothing apart from His kids asking Him to do it. **"You do not have, because you do not ask"** (James 4:2).

Prayer is the beginning of the solution to every problem and situation there may be. In prayer, we call to our Father to move whatever obstacle there may be that is causing the problem, or to put one up to prevent or stop one. It's like calling the plumber when your pipes are clogged and you've tried everything. The plumber won't come unless you pick up the phone, dial the number, and talk to him. God is waiting for us to ask Him for help. Then, when we do, we must trust Him to answer according to His will, not ours.

God Answers Prayers With One Of Three Answers: "Yes," "No," Or "Wait!"

"Wait" usually means, "Be patient, there is work to do first." I love it when it's a quick "Yes." A few years back I wanted a new couch, not just for the wanting, but we were meeting for church in our home and I needed more seating space. Our house had space challenges because it was 100 years old. After searching for weeks, I found the perfect couch. It was in a large, crescent shape, which could seat 7, even 8 people, if they were smaller. Problem was, the price tag was $1,200 more than I had.

I went to my Heavenly Father and I said, "Lord, you know I need a couch and You know why. This one is perfect, but I don't have enough money, so I am going to leave it up to you. I am OK with it if You say "No," and I will wait for another one. I trust You in this Lord." I was at peace giving it to over Him. (In the past, I would have tried to figure out a way to get what I wanted.) The next day, Mike was visiting a church and a woman he'd never seen before came to him and said, "I don't know you, but God told me to give you this money for your wife to buy a couch." It was $600. Mike was later telling someone what happened and they said they wanted in on it and gave him another $600. That was the $1,200 and off to the store we went.

That was a wonderful, quick answer, but the answer I got in my testimony in the beginning of this book was a "wait" answer. It was between two and three years after praying, "God, make Mike a godly man," and months of pain and agony before I saw the answer to that one. There was lots of work to be done in Mike and myself. I wanted a quick yes, but thank God, He knew everything that needed to be done and in what order. He wasn't in a rush. It had to be finished 100 percent for us to be able to walk in His will and effectively guide others in getting free from the same bondages in which we had spent so many years.

God, Teach Me To Pray!

All my years prior to that time my prayers were very shallow, consisting of before meals and in times of need. In that desperate time of need I didn't have a clue how to pray. I began to ask God to teach me to pray. I welcomed the Holy Spirit to lead me. As Jesus said in John 14:26, **"He (the Holy Spirit) will teach you all things."**

The Holy Spirit did teach and guide me each day. I learned how to pray as an intercessor. *Intercessory prayer* is when you are called (or it may be a group of people) to stand in the gap, believing for something or someone, and pray until it happens. For some people, this is a spiritual gift, and they always have someone or something they are believing for. Some, as I was, are gifted to intercede for a season. If you feel a grieving or a burden for someone, it is very probable that God is asking you to pray for that person, or situation, that you are grieved about.

My sister woke up one night and felt a great burden for a man she knew. She began to pray, asking for some revelation on how to pray. The Lord showed her a white truck. She began interceding for him regarding a white truck, for his alertness and protection, but mostly she let the Holy Spirit guide her in her prayers. The next day, as she talked with her friend, she told him about her dream. He informed her that a white truck had missed him by inches on the road that night. Her willingness to get up and pray saved his life. This is one example of how God uses people in intercession.

I Began To Use The Gift Of The Spirit Called Tongues

There will be times when you don't have a clue what to say in your prayers. We will never fully know the heart of God in different situations, so in order to know we are praying His will we must submit to the Holy Spirit's guidance. In my situation, when I didn't know what to say, or how to say it, I began to use the gift of the Spirit called tongues, which is a language between you and God. I received this gift when I had hands laid on me for the Holy Spirit's power, but I hadn't used it much. I now desired it eagerly as I was desperate to pray godly prayers and to hear from God. (See the footnote with verses at the end of this chapter.)

I learned there are times to pray quietly, loudly, on my face, on my knees, laid out flat before Him, walking, sitting, driving, or whatever I am led to do. I also learned that weeping, even groaning, is a powerful prayer weapon. Romans 8:26 says, **"Likewise, the Spirit also helps in our weaknesses. For we do not know what we should pray for as we ought, but the Spirit Himself makes intercession for us with groanings**

which cannot be uttered." Healing and cleansing comes with weeping and tears, and the tears aren't just for the ladies.

As you grow in your relationship with Christ it will become more and more natural to talk to God all day about everything. When serious prayer is needed, get in whatever position you feel like and ask for the Holy Spirit's guidance. Be willing to open your mouth and let out the words and utterances He is giving you.

3. WORSHIP

What is worship? In the original English it was pronounced "worth-ship," and the meaning is to give worth to something or "to acknowledge the one worshipped." Words to describe *worship* can include intense, or excessive devotion or regard, adoration, deep respect or reverence, to be in awe of. These definitions are very sobering to think about. When we worship, we are not just singing songs or speaking praises. Worship is respectfully acknowledging our King, being excessively devoted to Him, giving thanks for all He's done, and standing in awe of His greatness!

Why Do We Worship?

We worship to exalt Him above all else in our life. Psalm 148:13 says, **"Let them praise the name of the Lord, for His name alone is exalted, His glory is above the heavens and the earth."**

We worship so our prayers are heard. John 9:31 says, **"Now we know that God does not hear sinners; but if anyone is a worshipper of God and does His will He hears them."**

We worship Him because we are His sheep and He is our Creator. Sheep are under the direct guidance and protection of their shepherd. Psalm 95:6-7 says, **"Oh, come let us worship and bow down; let us kneel before the Lord our maker, For He is our God and we are the people of His pasture and the sheep of His hand."**

We worship Him because He is great, and worthy to be praised every day and we want to let others know of His goodness. Psalm 96:1-4 says, **"Oh sing to the Lord a new song! Sing to the Lord all the earth. Sing to the Lord, bless His name; Proclaim the good news of His salvation from day to day. Declare His glory among the Nations, His wonders among the people. For the Lord is great, and greatly to be praised."**

We worship to remember all that He has done for us, voicing our love, our thanks, and our adoration of Him. Hebrews 13:15 says, **"Therefore, by Him let us continually offer the sacrifice of praise to God, that is, the fruit of our lips, giving thanks to His name."**

It's In His Presence That We Become Like Him

We worship to get our minds off of ourselves and the drudgery of our daily lives and put our focus upwards to Him. By worshiping Him, we let Him know that no matter what our circumstances are, He is good and He is God and we are thankful for that. Psalm 148 emphatically states that everyone and everything created by God must worship Him.

Most of all, we worship because it is worship that brings us into His presence, and it's in His presence that we become more like Him. The portion of scripture that demonstrates this best is in 2 Chronicles 5:13-14. David had received plans from the Lord to build a temple, but God told David that he could not build it. His son, Solomon, would build it. In this scripture, the temple was finished and the Ark of the Covenant was being brought into the temple (in a moment you will read a very brief description of the Ark).

After the Ark was brought in, the people began to worship God. Verses 13-14 say, **"Indeed it came to pass, when the trumpeters and the singers were as one, to make one sound to be heard in praising and thanksgiving the Lord, and when they lifted up their voice with the trumpets and cymbals and instruments of music, and praised the Lord saying 'for He is good, His mercy endures forever', that the house, the house of the Lord was filled with a cloud, so that the priests could not continue ministering because of the cloud; for the glory of the Lord filled the house of God."**

Incredible! The presence of God came and filled the room and it was so powerful the priests couldn't even minister. They didn't need to as the presence would have been so profound healing would naturally come. I know people who have seen this in our present day and it changed them forever. This is rare in corporate worship and I'll tell you why. The key in that scripture is that it says they were singing and making music "as one." That means EVERYONE was in unity giving their full attention to God, undistracted praise and thanksgiving to Him and Him alone.

How Do We Worship?

Worship can be done in prayers of thanksgiving and songs of praise, and is most commonly known to be done in a church. But I have had some very intense worship all alone in my home when I come with a real heart after Him and intent on being in His presence. Worship can be given in many other creative ways and in any size group. I know people who worship and give glory to God through their painting, dancing, or serving one another with their God-given abilities. If you have a talent, it can and should be used as a form of worship; give God glory through it!

Many people worship with the raising of their hands toward heaven. You may wonder why they raise their hands. I had a new Christian ask me that and my answer was this: the raising of hands is done as an act of submission, telling God, "I humbly surrender myself to You! I'll go where you say go, and do what you say do."

Let's look at some ways that people in the Bible worshipped.

2 Samuel 6:13-23: This is the story of David and his men bringing the Ark of the Covenant back into Jerusalem. The Ark was an elaborately

built container made to carry the very presence of God. It carried the original tablets of the Ten Commandments and it was the center of Israel's worship. As David and his men were carrying the Ark back they went just six paces and it says in verse 14, **"Then David danced before the Lord with all his might."** Then they came into the city **"with shouting and the sound of the trumpet...David leaping and whirling before the Lord."**

Another favorite of mine is in Luke 7:36-38: **"And behold, a woman in the city, who was a sinner, when she knew that Jesus sat at the table in the Pharisee's house, brought an alabaster flask of fragrant oil, and stood at His (Jesus) feet behind Him weeping; and began to wash His feet with her tears and wiped them with the hair of her head; and she kissed His feet and anointed them with fragrant oil."**

I pick these two examples because they are completely different, and each is a beautiful example of worship. Neither David nor the sinner woman cared what people thought. The first time I did a teaching on worship, as I studied it I remember thinking, *I have judged people for doing things like this in the past.* David leaping and whirling before the Lord in public? During worship time at church, it can be so easy to judge others for how they are worshiping and be totally distracted so that we ourselves are unable to worship at all.

David's wife, Michal, made fun of him for his worship. You see, David was not only just dancing in public, but he took off most of his clothes and was wearing only his linen ephod. Basically he was in his undergarments. Verse 16 says she saw King David leaping and whirling before God and **"she despised him in her heart."** After David was finished worshipping, he made sacrifices and blessed all the people in the city.

Verse 20 says, **"Then David returned to bless his household, and Michal, the daughter of Saul, came out to meet David, and said** [very sarcastically I'm sure], **"How glorious was the king of Israel today, uncovering himself today in the eyes of the maids of his servants as one of the base fellows uncovers himself."** David's reply back to her was: **"It was before the Lord..., therefore, I will play music before the Lord and I will be even more undignified than this and will be humble in my own sight, but as for the maidservants you have spoken, by them I will be held in honor."** Here is an interesting part of the story: verse 23 says, **"Therefore, Michal, the daughter of Saul, had no children to the day of her death."** Her harsh judgment of David's form of worship did not please God!

I have a picture hanging in my home of David dancing in front of the Ark of the Covenant in his undergarments. I wanted this picture to remind me to be free in my worship, and unashamed before God. I will probably never dance in the street unclothed, but I try to remember to not inhibit my worship because someone might be watching and think I'm undignified.

The second example in Luke 7:36-50, the sinner woman came to Jesus convicted of her sinful life, worshipping Him at His feet. The hypocrites around Jesus judged Him for allowing her to do what she did, but He forgave her of her past sins and she left in peace. Now that's a beautiful and true worship experience! She came full of turmoil, worshipped the Lord, and left forgiven and full of peace.

The Spirit Of A Man Is The Lamp Of The Lord

John 4:24 says, **"God is Spirit, and those who worship Him must worship in Spirit and truth."** The Lord is looking for true worshipers. What does this mean? Mathew 15:8-9 says, **"These people draw near to me with their mouth, and honor me with their lips, but their heart is far from me and in vain they worship me."** God says we worship in vain when we say or sing praises to Him when our heart is not right before Him. True worship means to be real, to be honest, to be Spirit-led when you worship.

The spirit is the element in man by which he perceives, reflects, feels, and desires. The spirit is the element that gives him the ability to put his focus on God. Proverbs 20:27 says, **"The spirit of a man is the lamp of the Lord, searching all the inner depths of his heart."** It is God's Holy Spirit in us that gives us the desire to worship. When we were "born again," His Spirit began to reside in us. His Spirit shines the light on sinful things in our heart, which may hold us back from true worship. When the light exposes the sin in our heart, it brings conviction. Conviction is the feeling that we get when we see a wrong in ourselves, and we deeply desire to make it right before God. God is looking for those who will worship Him from the innermost depths of their heart. It is difficult to do this if your heart is not right before Him. Conviction is part of worship; it is the prelude to entering in, just like the sinner woman.

2 Corinthians 3:17 says, **"Now the Lord is Spirit, and where the Spirit of the Lord is there is liberty."** To have liberty means you are free from something. The Holy Spirit inside you convicts you of that sin in your life that holds you back from true worship. To get that liberty it's as easy as this: You feel the Holy Spirit's conviction, you repent, you're forgiven, it's done, and you're free from inhibitions. Now you can worship in truth, having integrity and sincerity in your worship, not just going through the actions. Whether you're alone or in a place of worship, you will sense more of the presence of God. (In a later chapter we will talk more about freedom from habitual sins).

Psalm 100 is called "A Psalm of Thanksgiving." It says, **"Make a joyful shout to the LORD, all you lands! Serve the LORD with gladness; Come before His presence with singing. Know that the LORD, He is God: It is He who has made us, and not we ourselves. We are His people and the sheep of His pasture. Enter into His gates with thanksgiving, And into His courts with praise. Be thankful to Him,** and bless His name. For the LORD is good; His mercy is everlasting, And His truth endures to all generations."

Worship Is Not Circumstantial

We are to acknowledge that God is good in the bad times as well as the good. In 2 Samuel 12:15-23, David had a child, and this child was conceived out of David's sin with Bathsheba, as told in chapter 11. God struck the child with illness and David pleaded with God through fasting and prayer for the child's life, but God allowed the child to die. David's servants told him the child was dead and David (verse 20) **"arose from the ground, washed and anointed himself and changed his clothes; and he went into the house of the Lord to worship."**

David, immediately after his child died, went to let God know that he still believes that He is good and worthy to be praised, even when his heart was in such pain! In our difficult times we can become bitter or better. We become bitter by focusing on the problem and asking, "Why me God?" We become better by choosing to trust God and praise Him no matter how bad it seems or how much pain we feel.

During my separation from Mike, all I felt like doing was crying and dying. My marriage and lifelong dream were both dead. I came to a point, after a few weeks, that I began to be thankful that God trusted me and loved me enough to allow such pain in order to draw me into His will. He knew that I could handle it and I become stronger and godlier through it. I was able to praise Him in the midst of my agony, knowing He was good, and only I could let my situation destroy me.

Romans 8:28 says, **"We know that all things work together for good for those who love God, to those who are called according to His purpose."** Ever since I was a child, this verse has been the foundation of my trust in God. I have never asked God "Why?" in any situation, because I know He will work it out for my good. I have seen Him do it many times! We must make the choice to praise Him no matter what!

Notes:

Verses on tongues to study: Mark 16:17; Acts 2 is the first account of the indwelling of the Holy Spirit; Acts 19:6; 1 Corinthians 14:2, 14, and 39. I also recommend a small book by David VanCronkhite called *A Supernatural Language in a Supernatural Kingdom*. The Web site is: www.bloodnfire.com.

– 6 –

WALKING IN RIGHTEOUSNESS

How Is It Possible To Be Righteous?

The word "righteous" seems so holy, so unattainable. It seems as if only God can be righteous. If you feel that way, you really don't understand what it means to be righteous or to walk in righteousness.

Righteous means to *be in right standing with God*; it does not mean you are sinless. First, I will do my best to explain how it is possible to be in right standing with God.

Genesis 1:27 says, **"God created man in His own image, in the image of God."** We were created to be in His image and likeness. We are the only creation *God breathed His own life into*! Adam and Eve were created perfect, sinless, LIKE GOD, and they were righteous and Satan knew this. When Satan, in the form of a serpent, tempted Eve, he did it using the same lie he himself fell for.

Isaiah 14:12-14 records Satan's thought process before his fall from heaven. It says he thought, **"I will be like the Most High."** He used the same lie to tempt Eve. Satan said to Eve, **"For God knows that in the day that you eat of it your eyes will be opened, *and you will be like God*, knowing good and evil"** (Genesis 2:5, emphasis added). They didn't grasp that they were already as close as they could get to being like God.

When Eve ate of the fruit, then gave Adam to eat, which was the first sin, it brought instant shame. Genesis 2:8 says, **"They heard the sound of the Lord God walking in the garden in the cool of the day, and Adam and his wife hid themselves from the presence of the Lord God among the trees in the garden."** (They didn't know yet that you can't hide from God.)

For the first time, Adam and Eve felt ashamed of their nakedness. Satan knew that not only would this act bring shame, but it would also take away their constant communion with God. In the garden they had complete access to God at all times. After the sin, the Lord placed cherubim (angels) at the entrance of the garden. Adam and Eve were no longer righteous, and communion with God now had to be initiated by God.

I spoke earlier that before Christ's death, a priest needed to offer a sacrifice for sins. Also, before His death and resurrection, it was only the High Priest who was allowed to go into what was called the "Holy of Holies." The "Holy of Holies" was the place in the temple, behind a veil, where only the High Priest, after ritualistic cleansing, could enter and meet with God's presence. It was like going through the cherubim into the garden again.

When Christ breathed his last breath on the cross, Mathew 27:50-51 says, **"Behold the veil of the temple was torn in two from top to bottom."** This was not an act of man, but God, and it represented that Christ's death made the presence of God accessible again to all of us who are His children. No longer did we need the priest, we can go directly to God with our request. When we were "born again," the old unrighteous man died (Adam represents that old, sinful-natured man). We were recreated at that moment and made righteous in our Holy Spirit nature, just as Adam was originally created; only Adam lost it and could never earn that righteousness back.

We also could not earn it, but 2 Corinthians 5:21 tells us, **"For He made Him who knew no sin, to be sin for us, that we might become the righteousness of God in Him."** Christ, who was sinless in every way, bore our sins that we may become righteous (in right standing with God), and enter into God's presence anytime we wish to do so.

(If you wish to read a few more verses on our righteousness, here are a couple you can to look at: Romans 3:9-18 speaks that in the law, righteousness was unattainable, and verses 21-22 tells us that in the new covenant, through our faith in Jesus, we are righteous; Galatians 2:19-21 says that we died to the law and are righteous through Christ who lives in us.)

How Do I Walk In Righteousness?

1 John 3:7 says, **"Little children, let no one deceive you. He who practices righteousness is righteous, just as He is righteous."** What does it mean to "practice righteousness"? Like anything you wish to be good at, you must practice. If you want to be a great piano player, you must spend many hours a day, for many years practicing. Great football players, actors, or business people don't get to be great without experience, and when they make a mistake they get back on their feet and do it over. Walking in righteousness is the same, and this is where the Holy Spirit's conviction, along with God's grace, is a beautiful and necessary process.

Gods Grace Is Very Simply God's Favor
That We Don't Deserve And Cannot Earn

When Christ was getting ready to go to heaven, He said, **"I tell you the truth, it is to your advantage that I go away; for if I do not go away the Helper will not come to you; but if I depart I will send Him to you. And when He comes He will convict the world of sin and of righteousness and of judgment: Of sin because they do not believe in Me, of righteousness because I go to my Father and you see me no more and of judgment because the ruler of this world is judged....**

When He, the Spirit of truth has come He will guide you into all truth" (John 16:7-11).

In this portion of scripture, Christ explains the job of the Holy Spirit: 1) Convict the world of their sin; 2) Convict His own of their righteousness (this is where we are going to focus); 3) Convict of the coming judgment of Satan; and 4) the Holy Spirit came to guide us into the truth. When I previously wrote about the Holy Spirit's conviction, I want you to understand that the purpose of that conviction is not to make us feel bad about our sin. The purpose is to remind us that we are **not** sinners anymore, WE ARE RIGHTEOUS! He convicts us of our righteousness.

Let's say you're going down that road to maturity in Christ and you get distracted by your old self, a desire that is not godly. It is the Holy Spirit's job to speak to your mind and say, *"Hey, don't go there, ...recalculate... turn around and get back on the right track."* Now it is up to you to listen or ignore that voice. You will fail sometimes, and the old law (or the enemy) would say to you, "You sinned, and you must not sin! You are a bad Christian. You can't be righteous!" But your spirit says, "You are righteous! That sinful nature is not who you are anymore!"

Your soul must be trained, through practice, to walk in righteousness. You have to learn to focus on who and what you are – righteous – and not what you can't do or who you used to be. When you do or say something sinful, receive God's grace, get back on the right path, and know that you are in right standing with God!

As a loving parent, when I watched my children learning to walk, I would stand in front of them and encourage them, "Come to Mommy, you can do it!" Often they would fall on their way to me. I would not say, "YOU STUPID KID! CAN'T YOU DO ANYTHING RIGHT?" No, I would say, "It's okay. Come on, let's try again. Come on, get up, you can do it!" They never gave up, and all of them, with practice, learned to walk right.

That is how God's grace is for you. He's bidding you to come closer to Him, and when you get distracted and fall, He will be there to help you get up and try again. You will get better and better as you continue to practice. If you focus more on the discouragement of the enemy and give up, you will always be a crippled, stagnant, dysfunctional Christian, a sleeper.

Doing Good Works Will Not Make You Righteous

Romans 9:30-32 says, **"What shall we say then? That Gentiles who did not pursue righteousness, have attained to righteousness, even the righteousness of faith; but Israel pursuing the law of righteousness, has not attained to the law of righteousness. Why? Because they did not seek it by faith, but as it were by the works of the law. For they stumbled at that stumbling stone."** This scripture is telling us that the

Gentiles attained righteousness through faith; they simply believed. The Israelites pursued it, yet could not attain it, because they were trying to gain it through the works of the Old Testament law.

Romans 10:3 says, **"For they (Israelites) being ignorant of God's righteousness, and seeking to establish their own righteousness, have not submitted to the righteousness of God. For Christ is the end of the law for righteousness to everyone who believes."** Verses 9-10 say, **"If you confess with your mouth the Lord Jesus Christ, and believe in your heart that God raised Him from the dead, you will be saved. For with the heart one believes unto righteousness, and with the mouth confession is made unto salvation."**

Here is the whole key to righteousness: IF WE UNDERSTAND AND BELIEVE THAT WE ARE RIGHTEOUS, THEN IT IS NATURAL TO WALK IN RIGHTEOUSNESS! We then are not focused on our sin, but on the fact that we are in right standing with our Lord. As it says in Romans 6:11, **"Reckon yourselves to be dead indeed to sin, but alive to God in Christ Jesus our Lord."** 1 Corinthians 15:34 says, **"Awake to righteousness, and do not sin."**

Remember, the old you is DEAD! Is does not matter how "bad" you were. Forget what lies behind and press on to righteousness. When you stumble and say or do something out of the character of God, keep your trust in Him. He will help you up and give you the strength to get beyond your faults, try again, and stay on the path of righteousness. And you will become more like our Lord each day.

The more time you spend with God (perfect righteousness), the more sensitive you will be to unrighteousness.

7

RENEWING THE MIND
AND RULING OVER SIN

My mind is the soil,
In which my thoughts take in seed,
What I see, hear and think,
Will through my mouth and actions proceed.

In Genesis 4:3-5, Cain and Abel, the first two sons of Adam and Eve, both brought the Lord a sacrifice. The Lord was pleased with Abel's, but not Cain's. This made Cain very angry. It says in Genesis 4:6-7, **"So the Lord said to Cain, 'Why are you angry and why has your countenance fallen? If you do well will you not be accepted and if you do not do well, sin lies at the door, and its desire is for you, but you should rule over it.'"**

This was a strong warning given to Cain that sin was lying in wait to destroy him. The very next verse tells how Cain handled this warning: **"Now Cain talked with Abel, his brother; and it came to pass when they were in the field, that Cain rose up against his brother and killed him."** Now that was completely ignoring the voice of God. Today we have the Holy Spirit's conviction. Cain had God speak right to him and warn him. So what did he do? He let sin rule him and he KILLED his brother.

James 1:14-15 says, **"But each one is tempted when he is drawn away by his own desires and enticements. Then when desire has conceived, it gives birth to sin; and sin, when it is full grown, brings forth death."**

When God gave Cain that warning, sin had most likely already conceived. Where does sin conceive? In our mind, of course. Our mind is the soil that takes in the seed; therefore, our mind is the place we must take the most precaution with and recognize ahead of time what's going in. In Cain's case, he let his mind conceive and he gave birth to it when he acted on it. This act brought forth death to his brother and himself in very vital areas of his life (verses 11-12).

As Christians we walk in different places. We each have a different area where sin may "lie at the door," but it always starts in the same place: in our thought process. All temptation to sin is birthed in our human soul. Soul in Hebrew is *Nephesh*, which means self, mind, personality, inner desires. It is our mind, will and emotions. In our soulish realm, we look at sin and think that it will be pleasant and we desire it. Just like Eve in Genesis 3:6, **"When the woman saw that the tree was good for food, that it was** *pleasant* **to the eyes, and a tree** *desirable* **to make one wise, she took of the fruit and ate."** Sin always seems pleasurable and desirable at the time, and it may appear as if there are no repercussions at first, but if you continue in sin, ignoring the Holy Spirits convictions, you will, over time become insensitive to those convictions. Your righteousness will begin to die and your soul will again become dominant in your life. This is how it brings forth death to your spirit.

Christians walk at different levels of maturity and victory. There are three general levels:

1. The Backslider (Soul Dominates)

This Christian, at one time genuinely accepted the Lord, maybe had some change at first, but over time became lazy about their growth, (maybe due to lack of knowledge). They may pick up their Bible from time to time out of duty, not really desiring the responsibility of understanding what it says. They begin, over time, to give in to their weaknesses again and again and have slowly become insensitive to the Holy Spirit's convictions and anything spiritual. They may or may not still go to church. They may say they are Christians, but God is obviously not a priority in their daily living.

2. The "Stagnant" Christian (Spirit And Soul Battle It Out)

This Christian goes to church, claims to be a Christian and talks the talk. They know a lot about God's word and Christianity. They probably are leaders in the church and may frequently read the Word. The problem is, they never ask God to reveal their weaknesses because they don't think they have any; therefore, they never change and grow.

The sin in their life is unrecognized because it's not the biggies, like stealing, murder or adultery. Their sin is more likely to be gossip, criticism, and judgment of others. They never get victory, because they usually see other's sin as worse than their own. They haven't turned away from God; they just haven't learned to heed the Spirit thoughts over the soulish thoughts. They never get to know Him and their overcoming power through Him. Because they think other people's sins are worse than theirs, they see themselves as more "spiritual" than others. This was me. For many years I thought I was more mature than most Christians. Now I tell people, "The more mature I become as a Christian, the less mature I **think** I am!"

Unfortunately, it usually takes some serious pain to get a stagnant Christian to realize their deep need for inner change enough to do something about it. The Bible calls this the "lukewarm" Christian (Revelation 3:15-16). They can be hot for God when convenient, but in their daily life they are pretty cool. God is on their mind a lot, but there is always something else that takes priority.

3. The Ever Maturing Or Righteous (Spirit Dominates)

This Christian is daily aware of their weaknesses, and is always seeking God's strength to change them. They have learned how to rule over sin by continually choosing to divert their wrong thoughts and not allow them to conceive into sin. When they mess up, they quickly seek and receive God's grace and get back on the path of righteousness. They are much less likely to judge others because they understand the grace God has had for them. They have a continual hunger to know Him; therefore, they read out of desire and love for God, not obligation. God is their constant companion and they are growing and becoming more Christ-like daily.

Awake, You Who Sleep!!

I call the first two levels the "living dead," because they have accepted God at one point, so their Spirit did get AWAKENED, but they allowed it to go back to sleep. To those of you in that place, please let me say emphatically, Ephesians 5:8, **"For you were once darkness, but now you are light in the Lord. Walk as children of light."** You gave your heart to God; therefore, you are not darkness as you once were. Your spirit has gone back to sleep and You ARE the living dead. Please hear this loud and clear: Ephesians 5:14 says, **"WAKE, you who sleep, ARISE from the dead, and Christ will give you light."** Tell your spirit to WAKE UP! And come to the forefront again! Then please keep reading.

The major difference in your level of maturity and victory comes from how much control of your mind you have. Romans 12:2 says, **"Do not be conformed to this world, but be transformed by the renewing of your mind, that you may prove what is that good and acceptable and perfect will of God."** If all sin is conceived in the mind, then the only way to combat it is to renew the mind. That is how we are transformed from sinner, backslider, or stagnant, into the ever-maturing righteous!

How Do I Renew My Mind?

The first and most important step in the process of being renewed is to realize your ability to "CHOOSE."

Deuteronomy 30:19 says, **"I have set before you life and death, blessing and cursing; therefore CHOOSE LIFE, that both you and your descendants may live."** This verse should be applied to any thought that comes into your mind. Ask yourself if the thought gives life or will it bring spiritual death? Then you make your choice. It may be a thought of sin, which seems as if it will be pleasurable; or it may be a thought from the past, which torments you.

The enemy begins at a very young age to plant lies about ourselves in our minds. If you listen to them, over time you believe them. It might have been that you're ugly, you're no good, you're not sexually normal, or you're stupid. Whatever negative thought it was, it was a lie you received and over time you believed it. The lie may have just been in your mind, or the enemy may have used someone to tell you the lie or did things that made you believe it.

Every thought, whether sinful or a lie you've believed, is your choice to dwell on or to replace with another thought. Not just any thought, a life-giving one. Philippians 4:8 says, **"Whatever things are true, whatever things are noble, whatever things are just, whatever things are pure, whatever things are lovely, whatever things are of good report, if there is any virtue, and if there is anything praiseworthy, meditate** (think hard) **on these things."** You have the power to change your thoughts anytime you choose, give it to Christ and think on something praiseworthy.

1 Corinthians 2:16 says, **"We have the mind of Christ,"** so you can think like Him! I have spoken in a group setting about how easy it is to change a thought. I asked everyone to stop listening to me for a minute and count to ten out loud. When they got to about 5, I abruptly said, "Stop!" and they immediately stopped counting and looked at me. Then I said, "See how easy it is to stop what you are thinking and redirect your thought?" and they got it. This does take practice as our mind has been allowed to roam freely for so long.

Your mind produces thoughts based on what you believe, what you have focused on, and what you have kept in tune with. Say you were abused as a child. That abuse can rule you if you keep your thoughts there. I don't want to make light of abuse, but if you choose to change your focus to what God's plan for your life is rather than how the enemy destroyed it, you will begin to heal and God will begin to use you. The enemy can only destroy your life if you let him. As you choose to redirect your focus and tune in to God's thoughts vs. the enemies, your mind changes and becomes more sensitive to the Spirit than to the wrong thoughts the enemy has kept you bound up in.

When you first become aware of your *ability* to control your thought process, that is when you make your choice to begin to take control of your thought life. Then you should start with the area that you struggle with the most, and when a thought comes, give yourself another more pure one that is life giving. If whatever you struggle with has been a stronghold in your life for a while, you may need an accountability friend to encourage you and help you along. I will give two good examples I know of how a deprived mind can be transformed and trained to think differently.

When my husband Mike returned from his backslidden state and recommitted his life to the Lord, he had to renew his mind. His mind had been allowed to roam into perverted thoughts for so many years that it was natural for it to go there. He now desired righteousness and when his mind went there he had three godly friends he could call as soon as the thoughts would come. He would call one and say, "I need prayer right now for my mind." If he couldn't get hold of one, he would call the next one, until someone prayed with him. He was diligent and eventually he was strong enough to take control of his own thoughts. He learned what the triggers were to the thoughts and how to avoid them. Over time, it became no longer natural for his mind to wonder to perverted thoughts. He had retrained his mind to focus on more pure and righteous thoughts.

The next example is also from Mike's life. This story shows how far a mind can go, yet become pure again, through choice. When we were separated, and for a while before that, Mike grew to hate me. In my testimony I shared how my kids and I began to attend an inner-city church. When Mike found out the area where the church was located, he found himself wishing I would be raped and killed. If you knew Mike, you would know how shocking that is. Even if you don't know him, it's shocking. You see, he thought I was the obstacle standing in the way of his freedom and he wanted me out of his way so bad, he figured the only way was to have me out of the picture. That way there would be no legal issues for him; no child support, no spousal support, and no pressure to restore a relationship because I would not exist.

These horrible thoughts were all fruit of a mind allowed to go anyplace it wanted to, just like the pornography. Satan is the father of lies and he will plant all sorts of them in your head if you allow him to. The more self centered you are, the more likely you are to focus on them.

He Had To Completely Renew All Thoughts

Now put these two examples together. Both were situations of a mind out of control, which brought destruction to our lives. Mike then made his choice to return to God, move back home and restore our marriage and family. He had to completely renew all his thoughts, the perverted ones and his thoughts and feelings toward me. He did not love me when he moved home, but he made the choice that he would love me again and began to confess it. When ungodly thoughts came in, he would choose to redirect his mind.

Just like on the highway with the GPS, he had to make his mind recalculate, turn around and go back to pure and praiseworthy thoughts. 2 Corinthians 10:5 says that we are to **"bring every thought into captivity to the obedience of Christ."** Mike said it took about two weeks of thinking, confessing, and acting as if he loved me (out of obedience to Christ) before he began to feel love for me again. This took courage, discipline, and faith on his part, and it paid off greatly for my man of God and for myself.

Your Past Will Rule You As Long As It Is Your Focus!

Mike and I don't dwell on the past. He doesn't beat himself up for being so ungodly and unfaithful and I don't ever put it in his face to shame him. And he doesn't remind me of my past controlling ways. We repented, forgave each other, and choose to look to our future in peace. The enemy did, and still does from time to time, try to bring bad memories into remembrance. I have to tell him to SHUT UP! I remind him who we are in Christ and that he could not take away what God has done!

I have been counseling a woman for years who was horribly abused as a child. She has shared and we've talked and prayed many times. She was still bringing it up too much and dwelling on it daily. I know that with abuse it can be a lifetime of living it over and over, but it doesn't have to be. I said to her one day, "If you are driving your car always looking in the rear view mirror at what's behind you, you're going to crash, guaranteed! Your past will rule you as long as it is your focus. Look ahead! Look forward!"

Trust God to heal all memories and switch your focus to your future! Think on what God's plan for your life is today, tomorrow, and the rest of your life!

Put On, Put Off!

Our spiritual growth and freedom from our past always comes as we make daily choices. In Colossians 3 we read, *"Seek* **those things which are above...***set* **your mind on things above...For you died and your life is hidden in Christ...,** *put to death* **your members which are on the earth; fornication, uncleanness, passion, evil desire and covetousness, which is idolatry....in which you once walked, but now you are to** *put off* **all these: anger, wrath, malice, blasphemy and filthy language out of your mouth. Do not lie to one another, since you have** *put off* **the old man with his deeds and have** *put on* **the new man who is renewed in knowledge according to the image of Him who created him.... Therefore,** *put on* **tender mercies, kindness, humility, meekness, longsuffering; bearing with one another and forgiving one another.... But above all** *put on* **love, which is the bond of perfection...***let* **the peace of God rule in your heart...***let* **the word of God dwell in you richly"** (emphasis added).

This scripture is a beautiful example of how we become more like Christ. Set your mind to godly things, (we do that through prayer, study and worship). Put off (get rid of) the bad, put on the good, and let the word of God and the peace of God dominate your life! As we study and let the words dominate us, we learn the mind of Christ, and it becomes more natural for us to think as He thinks, pure and lovely.

When I struggle with my mind and need new thoughts, I get my Bible out, find scriptures pertaining to whatever the problem may be. Then I read it over and over. I also print it up and tape it somewhere that I will see it often. I study it for however long it takes for me to get it sunk in my mind deep enough that I have victory. No other thing will transform our mind like the word of God.

These are things we make up our mind to do. No one can do it for us. As we do them, it gets easier and easier. Just as the wrong thoughts produce bad fruit, the right thoughts will begin to produce good fruit in our life. Mike, through making the choice to set his mind on things above and disciplining himself, became that man of God that God promised me! His desire was to be righteous and to love God first, then family. The fruit was and is evident.

He is a servant and loves to give, which is what God uses him to do in such a big way all over the world. He is kind to me in every way and makes his love for me clear to all. He willingly and frequently shares his past sins and victories to encourage others that they too can be free from strongholds in their mind and life. Our marriage gets stronger every year and our love for God and each other gets deeper. We like to tell each other, "You are my favorite person in the whole world."

On the other hand, what happens when we don't set our mind on things above? Every clock has a power source, whether it is a battery, electricity, or wind up. When it needs a new battery or winding, it begins to move a little slower, which lets you know it needs a boost. If you choose to ignore it, it eventually dies.

This is how Christians become stagnant or backslidden; they have neglected their power source. They have not "put off the old and put on the new." *The only clock that never slows or dies is the one with an electrical cord that keeps it continuously connected to the power source.* When you were "born again" and breathed your first spiritual breath, that was only the beginning. You became connected to the power source. A newborn babe needs more than that first breath to keep living and growing. A babe needs food and care or it stops growing and would eventually die.

The difference between newborn babe and a newborn Christian babe is that the human babe cannot get its own food and care. The newborn spirit babe is responsible to get their own food and care by getting involved with a church and seeking God daily, the power source.

The backslider either has not connected or has quit connecting with his food source; therefore, no power is left in him and he dies spiritually. The "stagnant" person only connects enough to survive.

The "ever maturing" stays connected, feeding their spirit continuously and allowing God to care for them through the thick and thin of life, therefore, growing each day toward Christ-likeness.

The really good news is that the backslider, such as Mike was, or the stagnant, such as I was for many years, can always reconnect. It took God allowing desperate times for us to get ourselves reconnected, but it has had lifetime effects. Our hearts and minds are both set on righteousness and our lives are full of joy and peace, even in the worst of times that we go through.

Romans 8:5-6 says, **"For those who live according to the flesh, set their minds on things of the flesh, but those who live according to the Spirit, the things of the Spirit. For to be carnally minded is death, but to be spiritually minded is life and peace."**

"My Prayer"
By Roxy Lynch

My life is completely
Committed to you
My mind, my mouth
And all things that I do

My failures are many
Each and every day
You lovingly forgive them
And redirect my way

My heart yearns to be like You
And learn how to love
Fill me with more
Of Your anointing from above

Empower me with ability
To guide others to you
To speak words that will heal
And bring maturity too

I trust You my Lord
With my life in Your hands
I will go where You lead me
Be it home or other land

My life, my whole life
I submit to Your keep
My prayer is to daily walk
Bowed down at Your feet

8

STRONGHOLDS

2 Corinthians 10:4-5 says, **"For the weapons of our warfare are not carnal, but mighty in God for pulling down strongholds, casting down arguments and every high thing that exalts itself against the knowledge of God, bringing every thought into captivity to the obedience of Christ."**

A stronghold is anything that has a strong hold of your mind keeping you in bondage to sin or ungodly behaviors. We are to take every thought captive, as the mind is where strongholds are established. They are established through fear and a false belief and will keep you blinded to the truth; therefore it is difficult to see your own strongholds, yet others may see them clearly.

For example, I shared how I didn't know how to love in my younger days, but I wanted everyone to show me they loved me. This was evidence of a stronghold of rejection. I never felt loved as a child; therefore, I believed the lie that I must be unlovable or difficult to love. I didn't want to put myself in the vulnerable position of showing love to someone only to be rejected. These thoughts led me to that desire I shared about in my testimony: the desire to be the perfect wife and mother and to have the perfect family where everybody loved each other.

In verse 5 of 2 Corinthians 10 it says, "...**casting down arguments and every high thing that exalts itself against the knowledge of God."** God wanted a total transformation of my thoughts and I was determined to get just that. It was against the knowledge of God for me to need perfection around me to make me feel secure. I needed to bring those thoughts into captivity and make sure my deepest desire was to draw nearer to Christ and make Him my priority. Therefore my security would come from Him, not Mike or my kids.

I did this by paying close attention to His faithfulness, reading His word daily, and being obedient to what it said. I began to believe that He loved me. I began to get free from the lies and receive His love and love Him in return. In the process I was learning that through Him I was lovable. I then began to love myself and so became capable of loving others without fear of rejection.

Instead of thinking, *How can Mike show me he loves me?* I would try to think of ways I could show him I loved him. This was a process that took time. Now I can sincerely love God, Mike, and everyone else, even if people do reject me.

All of us know someone who is always right (in their opinion). To a secure person, an argument may seem of no consequence because who cares who's right? But a person who has a stronghold of insecurity has a great need to be right as it makes them feel they are important or smarter than others. My dad was a great example of this. First, let me say that all my siblings and I have forgiven my father for all his dysfunctional words and actions and we have chosen to love him.

My dad lived a life of lies. He believed that he knew everything, he could do everything better than anyone, and nobody else knew the things he knew. He never admitted the horrible wrongs he did in life. I don't think he ever believed that he did them; it was always somebody else's fault. My dad was the most prideful and bitter man I knew. As a child I HATED him, but as I grew strong in my walk with God I became aware of the roots (where the pain stemmed from) in his emotional bondage. I realized it was severe insecurity and fear that drove him to such pride. This fear and insecurity became a stronghold in his life at a very young age. It was as if he was fighting against the world, standing in his corner ready to swing.

His Stronghold Stripped Him Of His Anointing

My dad passed away a year before I started writing this book. In his last days my sisters and I needed to care for him full-time. We all knew that many years prior he had committed his life to the Lord, but we never saw a bit of evidence of that salvation. In those last days we all asked him if he was right with God. He was very perturbed that we would ask, as we should know.

His stronghold kept him in bondage about many things, such as reading the Bible. He said he didn't need to read the Bible because God spoke directly to him. He didn't need to pray because God answered all his prayers before he could speak them. In those last days I kept asking God for reassurance of his salvation. One day God spoke to us through a prophetic word given to my sister, Denise. This word said that "because of the sister's prayers, the family strongholds and bondages would go to the grave with your father." My father's stronghold of insecurity brought a bondage of anger, bitterness and pride, and it stripped him of his anointing, rendering him useless in walking out God's plan for his life.

My dad had lung cancer and his lungs were slowly filling up, making his breathing more difficult each day. One day, as he was near the end, the Lord urged me to drive the 60 miles to see him. The Lord wanted me to play a song for my dad and speak some words to him, so I drove to another sister's home where he was moved to for his last days because there were no hospice rooms available. When I arrived, it was clear it would not be long. I asked dad if I could play him a song and I put the headphones on his ears. The song was, "Yet I Will Praise Thee" and the words summarized are as follows:

"I will praise You Lord my God, even in my brokenness, even in my desperation... I can't understand all that You've allowed; I just can't see the reasons. And though I cannot see You, I choose to trust You. Even when my heart is torn and my world is shattered and it seems all hope is gone, I will praise Thee... even in my darkest valley I will trust You!!"

When the song finished, I told him, "Dad, God is about to restore the anointing that was stopped by the family strongholds." You see, these strongholds had affected his whole generation. We all struggled in some of the same areas (as it says in Exodus 34:7). When I finished, Dad turned to us and shared where he had hidden lyrics, as he called them, that he had written years ago. About and hour or so later, all five of his kids, some spouses, and most of his grandchildren, gathered around his bed and began singing to him. He breathed his last breath as we sang the hymn, "Great is Thy Faithfulness." The next day my sister, Sue, found his lyrics hidden behind a dresser, right where he said it was. It was written as follows:

"Wreck-Amended by God"

Personal life was a wreck
And then was repaired by God
I am here today as living proof
That my life has been a
Wreck, amended by God
I was on a collision course with God
Working for the Devil
Believe me, I was His very best He had doing the work
Gambling, drinking, chasing women, I did it all
Then I found the right to accept
God and Jesus as my personal Savoir
And once I made this commitment to Christ
I promised I would work 10 to 100 times as hard and long on
working for Christ
And I promised to tell the world of my experience
And then do the work of saving souls for Christ.

My dad, sadly, never walked out God's plan for his life. But those words let us know the heart that was hidden behind all that toughness. I believe he really meant those words, and later God showed me that Dad never understood he had strongholds on his life, let alone knowing how to be free from them. We must be aware of them before we can be free.

I believed God's word that we, Dad's children, were now free from that stronghold. A few months later it was evident to me that I still had some anger issues and I had to personally confront them. I was free, but I still needed to make the choice not to let it consume me. That day I decided I would not allow it to happen. Many times during that particular day, I felt anger coming and I would say, "I WILL NOT BE ANGRY, the peace of God dwells in me!!" The next day the same, but less, then less. I still have to remind myself sometimes that the anger is gone and I have peace, but someday soon it will be totally natural for me not to be angry.

My anger was never a big issue with anyone but Mike, and I believe that was because I had been so angry at my dad as a child. It went back to that need to be loved. I got offended by silly little things, believing the lie that if he loved me he would do this or that (that old stronghold was trying to rear it's ugly head again). One day God said to me, *"Roxy, stop getting offended by everything he does and believe the truth, that he loves Me and he loves you!"* Simply put and simply believed by me. Now when I feel anger beginning to rise up, I remind myself of those words God spoke and choose to believe the truth.

The best way to find out what your strongholds are is to ask God to reveal them to you. If your really serious, you can lay yourself out on the floor and tell God, "Here I am on your operating table; cut me open (spiritually) and do your work." Then be real still and quiet and listen to His voice, His revelations, and let Him shine His light on your issues. Ask Him to deliver you and then make the proper choices each day, choosing the way of life!

Recognize the enemy's lies; they will come to prevent you from getting free and recognizing the truth! Then, when you have successfully gotten free from one, which can take awhile, ask Him to reveal another and walk through the process again. The revelation of strongholds and the process of getting free has changed my life dramatically, probably more than any other truth I have walked through. I now don't blame others for things so easily and I try to see what issues inside of me may be causing a problem. If I find it's me, I deal with it. If I believe it may be the other person, or persons, I don't judge them. I realize they probably don't see or understand their own strongholds. I know there is probably a hurt behind it and I can love them unconditionally. As I have gotten free of many strongholds, I have more joy in my life than I ever thought I could.

The next chapter will reveal the repercussions of living life without choosing freedom.

9

WILDERNESS OR PROMISED LAND
WHERE WILL YOU END UP?

Exodus 3 records when God spoke to Moses in the burning bush. The Lord met him there to tell him He had seen what the Egyptians were doing to His people, the Israelites. The Egyptians were using the Israelites as their slaves, controlling and abusing them to build a stronger Egypt. God spoke to Moses and told him what His will for his (Moses') life was.

Moses was told that he was the man God had chosen to deliver His people from Pharaoh and the Egyptian people. God told Moses to tell the people that He, their God, was going to deliver them and bring them to a great land flowing with milk and honey (Exodus 3:15-17). Many incredible miracles were done to achieve this rescue, starting with plagues on the Egyptians and ending with the parting of the sea for the Israelites to escape (chapters 7-14).

The land God spoke of in that portion of scripture has always been called the "Promised Land" for one obvious reason: God promised it to the Israelites. The problem was that the people had to cross the wilderness to get there. On this journey, they continued to see God working miracles all along the way, yet the people complained and complained (Numbers 11). Yes, they had some struggles, and that's where their focus was, on the daily struggles, not on their promise given by God. I am going to summarize chapters 13 and 14 of Numbers and you can read it on your own if you wish.

Faith Or Fear?

When the Israelites came close to the land God promised, they sent their twelve tribe leaders to spy out the land to assess how great it really was and if they could take it by force. They discovered that it was really great! Ten of the men came back saying, the fruits are huge, but so are the people there. **"No way we can fight those giants, we are like grasshoppers in their sight"** (13:33).

Two men, Joshua and Caleb, came back and said in faith, **"Let's go up at once and take possession, for we are well able to overcome it."** The people decided to believe the ten. It says in 14:1-3, **"So all the congregation lifted up their voices and cried and the people wept that night and all the children of Israel complained against Moses, and the whole congregation said to them (whining), 'If only we had died in the**

73

land of Egypt! Or if only we had died in this wilderness! Why has the Lord brought us to this land to fall by the sword, that our wives and children should become victims? Would it not be better to return to Egypt?'"

The people, hundreds of thousands of them, all knew that God had promised this land to them, yet when things looked a little rough they completely lost all trust. They whined and complained, even wishing they had died back in Egypt. They decided to elect a new leader to bring them back to Egypt. Joshua and Caleb tore their clothes in agony and tried again to convince the people: **"If the Lord delights in us then He will bring us into this land and give it to us...only do not rebel against the Lord...do not fear the people of the land, for they are our bread; their protection has departed from them and the Lord is with us."**

Have you ever had a word from God or a feeling God was ready to do something in your life? Then out of nowhere bad things seem to come at you and you began to doubt God and lose your faith? It always seems as if it would be easier to go back to our bondage than to face the giants we need to confront in order to gain our freedom! That's where these people were, so we'll go on and see what happens to them.

Moses Begs For Mercy

After Josh and Caleb gave their faith statement, it says the people decided to stone them, but the glory of God showed up and saved them. Verses 12-20 tell us that the Lord was angry with His people and wanted to kill them all, but Moses convinced the Lord that that would look bad to the Egyptians. After all those miracles, then to get angry and let them all die would make God look foolish. Moses begs for mercy and God gives it, but... He promises that none of them will see their Promised Land, except His very special servants, Joshua and Caleb, because they followed Him fully. They will be the only two that will survive to see it.

The Lord said that because the rest of the people had complained so much, everyone would die in the wilderness except Joshua and Caleb and the children who were born in the wilderness, the ones the people said "would become victims." They too would live to see it, but all the rest would die before they came into the land. And as punishment for their complaints, they and their children would wander forty years in the wilderness. Verses 33-34 say: **"And your sons shall be shepherds in the wilderness forty years and bear the brunt of your infidelity until your carcasses are consumed in the wilderness. According to the number of days in which you spied out the land, forty days, for each day you shall bear your guilt one year, namely forty years and you shall know my rejection."**

God's promise was just that, a promise, and God keeps His promises. But the ten spies with the bad report brought fear to the people and they responded in that fear. Joshua and Caleb had faith and tried to speak that faith into the others to no avail. Of the hundreds of thousands of people, only two kept their eyes on God and His promise, not on the problems. In the end, Joshua and Caleb were the only ones not born in the wilderness who entered their Promised Land. Trust is everything!

Proverbs 3:5 says, **"Trust in the Lord with all your heart, and lean not on your own understanding; in all your ways acknowledge Him and He will make your paths straight."**

We Need Trials

Contrary to what some believe, God never promised that we would not have problems. The Bible is full of stories of God's people facing problems and teaching us how to handle them through their mistakes or right choices. We are told that we most surely will face problems. 1 Peter 4:12 says to not think it strange when you are in a fiery trial. John 16:33 says, **"In the world you will have tribulation; but be of good cheer for I have overcome the world."**

Tribulation means *pressure, oppression, stress, anguish* or *adversity*. Romans 5:3 tells us why we should be patient and trust God through it. **"Tribulation produces perseverance, and perseverance, character, and character, hope."** We actually need trials to produce godly characteristics and make us stronger. This does not mean God throws us problems just to see how we will handle them. No, GOD IS GOOD!

I don't have the answer as to why things are allowed to happen in our lives other than problems are usually either human made or satanic forces at work often through humans. I do know that we are promised that if we trust in Him through our problem, He will make the path clear. It is in the midst of the trial (wilderness) that our faith is tested. Through our choices, we decide if we go back to our bondage, remain in the wilderness, or if we face our giants and fight for our freedom, stepping into His plan for us.

Typically, we will go in and out of wilderness and Promised Land experiences, growing godlier along the way, if we make the right choices. My marriage separation was my deepest, darkest wilderness. I fought my way through with the determination that I would not let the enemy mess up God's plan. I won that battle and stepped into my promised land for that time.

Things were good and we seemed blessed for several years. Then I heard God warn me that things were about to get rough again and we entered another wilderness time that lasted three years. It was not as painful, yet very difficult. Both Mike and myself grow more in love with God and each other through each trial. Right now we feel as if we are in a promised land again, but we won't be taken by surprise if another wilderness time comes and teaches us even more. I know one thing: I WILL trust my God through it all!

Those Who Lack Faith Will Talk More About Their Problem Than About What God Is Going To Do

You may be in a wilderness right now. It may be a problem marriage, a problem child, or a stronghold of sin in your life. Maybe you've suffered the death of a loved one or abuse at the hand of a loved one. Whatever it is, you have a choice. You can wander around for months or years saying you want freedom or answers and never doing anything about it except complaining and blaming God for your problems. Or you can choose to do what I like to call "your stomp your foot on the ground moment," referring back to my testimony. You tell the Devil "ENOUGH! I will fight for my promise!" Then you choose to never, never look back, keeping your eyes fixed on Christ!!

Those who lack faith will talk more about their problem than what God is going to do. Faith declares the power of God in the midst of the problem. Do whatever it takes to get control of your thoughts and actions. Be determined to become better, and make it your priority to trust God until the death of your problem. Be patient and keep trusting no matter how long it takes.

If you think you've waited too long, know that Joshua and Caleb got their promise, but they had to wait 40 years to see it, all because of the sin of the others. If you trust through until the end, you will grow and mature. God will be able to trust you with more, allowing you to get closer and closer to His perfect will and destiny for you. If you do not trust and grow, you will live your life and die never fulfilling what God created you to do. So make your choice. Will you step out in faith? Or will you give in and get angry and bitter at God and others, which will cause you to wander in circles spiritually, remaining in your wilderness?

My dad was a prime example of a man who lived his life wandering in a wilderness of bitterness and anger and died having never fulfilled what God called him to do. We loved him and forgave him, but he did not leave great stories or memories for his generations. I know it is very painful to our flesh to be humble and getting free of any stronghold takes some humility. But the cost of pride is too high to risk our very life and calling and that of our generations.

— 10 —

KINGDOM LIVING
WILL YOU LET THE ENEMY
STEAL IT FROM YOU?

Jesus taught us to pray, "Your kingdom come! Your will be done! On earth as it is in heaven!!"

Your Kingdom Come!

A kingdom is a government or country headed and ruled by a King. Jesus says to pray those words, "Your kingdom come," but how is it possible for God's kingdom to come right here on earth, for Him and Him alone to rule? God will not come to earth and take rulership over us because He has given us free will to choose whether or not we want to live by His rules. The only way for God's kingdom to come to earth, here and now, is for us to live our lives as if He is our king, our one and only ruler. This is "kingdom living." Jesus said, "...the kingdom of God is within you" (Luke 17:21).

What Does "Kingdom Living" Mean?

Kingdom living means that we have given God absolute rule and reign of our life. What He says, goes. Just like a King and his kingdom, He makes the rules and we follow them. The difference being that God, as our king, makes rules out of his deep love for each individual person. Kingdom living is choosing to live each day with God at the center of every decision made, letting Him guide and control our steps. Kingdom living is your surrender and absolute yielding of all your life to Him! When we live this way, we are bringing His kingdom everywhere we go because He lives in us. We become KINGDOM REPRESENTATIVES!

Mathew 6:33 says, "Seek first the kingdom of God and His righteousness, and all these things will be added unto you." When we put Him first in our lives, walking in righteousness and letting Him rule us, He makes sure all our needs are taken care of. As Mike and I have decided to keep striving after His kingdom in our daily lives, we have seen Him take care of our every need. We have had some prosperous times, and I believe God loves to prosper the righteous (Psalm 35:27). But we have also had some very hard times. Times when we have to trust Him on a day-by-day basis, even though we didn't know where the money was going to come from for our tomorrow. He has always made sure our every need is supplied each day. ("Give us this day our daily bread.")

Romans 14:17 says, **"For the Kingdom of God is not eating and drinking, but righteousness, peace, and joy in the Holy Spirit."** Kingdom living will be evidenced in our lives by the righteousness, peace, and joy we walk in throughout the good and the bad. The enemy's plan is to place situations in our lives that will steal our righteousness, peace, and joy.

This book has all been written for the purpose of your spiritual growth and walking in His will (kingdom) each day. I would like to share a major, yet sometimes subtle, distraction the enemy uses, which will definitely keep you from walking in His will for you. Although any sin or distraction will keep us from Kingdom living, this is just one lesson God taught Mike and me, which I believe is vital for everyone.

A Lesson Learned

Job 33:14-16 says, **"For God may speak in one way or in another, yet man does not perceive it. In a dream, in a vision of the night, when deep sleep falls upon man, while slumbering in their beds, then He opens the ears of men and seals their instruction."**

Mike had a dream. In this dream, he and I were searching for a great pearl. We were told that in order to get the pearl we would have to go through some difficult ordeals. In the dream we stood at a cliff and were told that to find the great pearl, we would have to jump off this very high cliff, swim hard to get very deep, then find a cave deep down and go into it. We decided we wanted it, no matter the difficulty, so we went after it. We jumped off the cliff into the clear blue water, swam hard, using a lot of energy to get deep enough to find the cave.

Then we went into the cave and came up from the water where we saw it. It was a beautiful, huge pearl, but next to it stood a very large dragon. Mike saw a sword near him and instinctively picked it up and began to fight the dragon to get to the pearl. The harder he fought and the more intense the fight got, it seemed to be empowering the dragon. I was behind him screaming, "PUT DOWN THE SWORD!" Mike, fearing for our lives, kept swinging. I again screamed at him, "DROP THE SWORD!!" He said, "If I drop it, we will get eaten." I again insisted that he drop it. Finally Mike dropped the sword and the dragon immediately was rendered powerless and we were able the get the Great Pearl!

I searched the word and prayed about this dream. Here is the interpretation I received. Matthew 13:46-47 says, **"Again the kingdom of heaven is like a merchant seeking beautiful pearls, who when he found one pearl of great price, went and sold all that he had and bought it."** The pearl in the dream represents the kingdom living Mike and I desire in our daily life. The swim hard and go deep part meant that we would be walking through, and have walked through some great difficulties as we have chosen to put Christ front and center of our lives, and we have dug deep in His word for guidance.

It did take me a while to figure out why the sword empowered the dragon. A sword usually represents the Word of God, but in this case it was a negative thing strengthening evil. Within a month, we had two different prophetic people have a vision of us, which brought revelation. Twice it was told to us that there was seen (prophetically) many knives and swords in our back.

We knew where they were coming from because we had several people spreading misinformation from things misunderstood about us. The second time these knives and swords were seen in a vision was while Mike was in Mozambique with Heidi Baker's ministry, Iris Ministries. He had gone with Michal Ann Goll and Compassion Acts to bring food to the orphanages and audio Bibles to the pastors since most of them cannot read. Michal Ann, a precious woman of God who has passed away since that trip, saw these knifes and swords and told Mike, "The purpose of these swords and knives in your and Roxy's back is to steal the kingdom from you." She proceeded to prophetically remove them. After Mike shared this with me, I thought to myself, "How can anyone steal the kingdom from us?"

Then the Lord gave me another revelation. When Saul attempted to spear David in Samuel 18:11, why did he do it? Verse 8 tells us that Saul was upset that the people loved and revered David more than him and he said, **"What more can he have, but the kingdom? So Saul eyed David from that day forward."** Saul was angry and jealous and thought if he could just kill David, he would prevent him from getting his kingdom.

Through this revelation the Lord showed me that anytime someone says ill words about Mike or me and we defend ourselves in any way, we are picking up a sword and fighting a battle that is not ours. Just like the story I shared about David and Saul where David could have killed Saul, but instead he said, "Let the Lord judge between you and me."

There have been many times verbal attacks have come against us in an attempt to make us or the ministry be looked at in a negative way. We know we do not fight flesh and blood, but kingdoms and principalities. Yet sometimes we have felt justified in getting upset or having righteous anger because we were defending God or God's ministry. The truth is that anytime we pick up our sword in defense of an offense, we are empowering the enemy to take kingdom living from us.

Offenses are going to come, especially when we are in God's will. It says in 1 Samuel 18:14-15, right after Saul attempted the first time to spear David, **"And David behaved wisely in all his ways and the Lord was with him. Therefore, when Saul saw that he behaved wisely, he was afraid of him."**

People who are insecure and fearful tend to fear those who are not and may say things against them to try and build themselves up. Saul continued to attempt to kill David in many ways, but God's favor was always with David. David had opportunities to retaliate, but he did not give in to anger. He didn't even speak negative words about Saul. David chose to let God deal with Saul, and eventually He did, and David got the kingdom.

Offenses are a powerful tool of the enemy to catch us off guard and pull us away from what God has for us. It can be as small as someone looking at you the wrong way. Maybe they said negative words about you or did something hurtful to you. Regardless of how big or small the offense may be, think of it as a direct threat from the enemy. Remember, again, we don't fight against flesh and blood (Ephesians 6:12), but against spiritual forces, which drive people to do or say destructive, hurtful things. Almost every day there are subtle offenses that can be taken from simply a misunderstanding that people choose to believe.

When the offenses are not dealt with, they become bigger offenses. Big or small, all are an attempt to get you off course spiritually with anger, then into bitterness. Do not fight them in the natural; fight in the supernatural with forgiveness, love, and prayer. Colossians 3:12-14 tell us how a "new creation in Christ" will handle it: **"Therefore as the elect of God, holy and beloved, put on tender mercies, kindness humility, meekness, longsuffering; bearing with one another and forgiving one another; even as Christ forgave you, so you must also do. But above all things, put on love, which is the bond of perfection."**

Now, when Mike and I start to take offense by something someone does or says, we remind each other, "Don't let them steal your kingdom from you!" We can forgive and love the person, lay it down under Christ's feet and go on in God's will for our day and life. I am certainly not perfect, but I keep on in the process striving toward the goal one step at a time.

Just this morning God convicted me of complaining about a situation with someone I love. I was doing it without even thinking it was wrong. Complaining is taking up an offense and griping about it, which is sin. I was stepping out of Kingdom living for a while. I was greatly convicted, asked for forgiveness and did another study on complaining. As I read that verse in Colossians (above), I was reminded of how many times Christ has forgiven me and continues to so daily. I too, will forgive and forgive!

One Last Point On Kingdom Living

Mathew 19:24 says, **"And again I say to you, it is easier for a camel to go through the eye of a needle than for a rich man to enter the kingdom of God...with men this is impossible, but with God all things are possible."**

I personally don't take this scripture as meaning it is impossible for a rich man to get into heaven. I believe that it means it is difficult for him, or her, to walk in God's kingdom today, His way of thinking and His government instead of their own. Sometimes, especially in great business minds, it has become so natural to come up with great ideas that it's hard to see the need to get Kingdom ideas.

Let's not think with our natural minds. In our everyday life, in our businesses, in our families, let's get kingdom minded because we do have the mind of Christ. Let's not let any idol, money, or anything else keep us from thinking like Christ.

As we live kingdom lives, God begins to expand our kingdom and this is how His kingdom will come to earth... through us! Let's let Him live through us and control us. Don't' let the enemy steal God's Kingdom from you.

So, will you join the ever-maturing ranks and say with me:

"LET YOUR KINGDOM COME IN ME LORD!!
LET YOUR WILL BE DONE,
HERE ON EARTH, AS IT IS IN HEAVEN!!"

"I Want To Be Holy Like You"
By Roxy Lynch

I want to be holy like You
To be righteous in all I say and do

To be a kingdom representative
Everywhere I go
To seek justice and compassion
For both the high and the low

To walk in peace and joy
No matter the circumstance
Forgiveness and love
No matter the offense

To lift others up
And always see the best
To become stronger and wiser
Through every trial and test

When people are near me
I long for them to see
A reflection of Jesus
As they see and watch me

So I put a guard on my tongue
And over my mind too
That I will think and speak wisely
As I walk each day through

Summary

The word "Christian" unfortunately has begun to be thought of in a negative way. We have been thought of more as hypocrites than as those who love God and love people. We must begin to look at ourselves not as *just* a Christian, but as more of a disciple.

In Bible times there were many believers (Christians), but a small number of disciples. The Christians believed in Jesus, but the disciples made a willful decision to make following Jesus the priority in their life, and to follow Him wholeheartedly! They daily sat at His feet. They walked with Him, ate with Him, fellowshipped with Him, and were taught by Him daily for a few years. **Then,** they began to do likewise with others, walking out what they were created to do. Like Joshua and Caleb, the disciples went beyond proclaiming faith; they lived it. They stood out in a sea of "God's people." God took notice and honored them. We are still learning from their lives and the books they wrote.

We were all created for a purpose and have a God-given destiny. Walking out that purpose and destiny is way too exciting of an adventure to miss out on because we are bound up with strongholds and sin. We all have our reasons for being the way we are, but it is no excuse for us to stay that way. YOU CAN CHANGE!! You can change your world around you too! Some people don't believe that, or just don't want to believe it, because it takes too much effort. It does take effort and the fruit that follows makes it well worth it!

We make our destiny choice by how we live our lives each day. We can simply fit in with the crowd of believers wandering around in our wilderness and be stagnant. We can decide it's easier to slide back into our bondages, or...we can be one of the few who decide that we will make that decision to make Him our priority. If He is our priority we will make our schedule fit around Him, spending time with Him daily in study, worship, and prayer. As we get to know Him, we become strong and choose to face our giants, fight in trust for our freedom, becoming victorious, and stepping right into what we were created to do.

How long this takes is up to you and your determination to *not* give up. Once you make the right choice, draw mental lines (boundaries) beforehand that you WILL NOT cross, such as knowing what *not* to click on your computer, or what thoughts to not allow yourself to entertain. Seek answers to your issues in the Word and talk to God and others you trust. Be strong in keeping your soul in submission to your spirit.

Do not let the enemy control your thoughts and destiny anymore! You will be transformed as you renew your mind, redirecting the ungodly thoughts and dwelling on more pure ones. Remember you are *not* a "sinner." You are righteous!

It was Paul who, incidentally, was one of the worst sinners in the Bible as he ordered the horrendous murder of Christians. It was he who reminds us to **"AWAKE to righteousness"** (1 Corinthians 15:34).

Daily make the right choices in obedience and you will find yourself following God's lead right into your destiny. You will be living a life of righteousness, peace and joy no matter the circumstance. And that, my friend, IS the kingdom of God!

**FOR THE KINGDOM OF GOD
IS NOT EATING OR DRINKING,
BUT RIGHTEOUSNESS, PEACE,
AND JOY IN THE HOLY SPIRIT.**
(Romans 14:17)